The Great Canadian

Food Show

Recipes from the
popular television series

Chris Knight

Macmillan Canada
Toronto

First published in Canada in 2000 by
Macmillan Canada, an imprint of CDG Books Canada

Canadian Cataloguing in Publication Data

Knight, Chris, 1960–
    The Great Canadian food show : recipes from the popular
television series

Includes index.
ISBN 0-7715-7666-8

1. Cookery, Canadian. 2. Great Canadian food show (Television
program). I. Title.

TX715.6.K64 2000   641.5971   c00-930758-3

This book is available at special discounts for bulk purchases by
your group or organization for sales promotions, premiums,
fundraising and seminars. For details, contact: CDG Books Canada
Inc., 99 Yorkville Avenue, Suite 400, Toronto, ON, M5R 3K5.

1   2   3   4   5   TRANS-ML   04   03   02   01   00

Cover and text design by Counterpunch / Peter Ross
Black and white photographs provided by Chris Knight
Colour photographs by Mark Roy

Permission to reproduce Canadian aeronautical charts or portions
thereof has been granted by Geomatics Canada, Department of
Natural Resources © 2000

Macmillan Canada
An imprint of CDG Books Canada Inc.
Toronto

Printed in Canada

To Jennifer and Adam, the two most important people in my life; thanks for putting up with me through all of this.

Acknowledgements

In recording these acknowledgements it is impossible to separate the tv show from the book. Neither would have been possible without the commitment and dedication of all these wonderful people: Carlo Rota for breathing life into my idea, Trevor Grant for turning it into great tv, Al Magee for turning it into great stories, Joe Novak for giving me a shot in the first place, Adele Cardamone for her patience, Derek Diorio for getting me through some dark days, Jill Lambert for her support and contagious laugh, and Christine Overvelde for being my right hand. Layton Burton is one of the best shooters in the biz. Thanks to George and Dorothy Tompson for their sage advice on separating what was truly interesting from what was self-indulgent dross. Many, many thanks to the researchers, editors, sound recordists, production assistants, and a zillion others (you know who you are) who have contributed to the series and the book. None of this would have been possible if it were not for David Templin, Don Cummer, Wendy Zatylny, and Iain Mitchell, who believed in me and my dream when I needed them most. Thanks to Elvis Presley, who sustained me in my moments of doubt by proving you don't have to have a lot of talent to be successful. Thanks to the security guy at the Chateau Whistler for not throwing us out when he thought we were making a porno movie in Carlo's room (it's a long story).

Finally, thank you to all the wonderful people across Canada who let us tell their stories. You opened your doors and your hearts to us and we are better for it. You have given us memories to last a lifetime, and I hope we have done you proud.

Please accept my heartfelt apologies if I have overlooked anyone, but my publisher wanted this in a hurry . . . .

Contents

Foreword   vii

1 Heli-Hiking and the Canadian
Bar-b-que   1

Grilled Leg of Lamb   3
Grilled Asparagus and Pork Salad   4
Bar-b-qued Sardines   5
Lemon Grilled Zucchini   6
Bugaboo Couscous   6
Bar-b-qued Pineapple   7

2 The Quebec City Bistros   8

Tartare aux Deux Saumons   10
Confit de Canard, Pommes à l'Ail   11
Most Excellent Fish Soup   12
Lima Bean Salad   13
Apples with Cinnamon Calvados Cream   14
Saissie de Caribou aux Petits Fruits des Marais   15
Foie Gras à l'Armagnac   16
*Frivolité de Saumon Fumée au Poireau et Fromage
de Chèvre*   17

3 Lac Portage and the Hunt for
Moby Trout   18

Pumpkin Soup   19
Truite en Colère avec Sauce Beurre Blanc   20
The Nutty Trout   22
Grilled Sea Bass with Watermelon-Mango
Salsa   24

4 Seasons in Thyme   25

Chicken Ballentine with Carrot Butter and Beet
Emulsions   26

Asparagus Soup with Chive Oil   28
Stefan's Mushroom Flan   29

5 Adventures in Chinatown   30

Thai Spicy Coconut Soup (*Tom Kha Gai*)   32
Vietnamese Beef and Shrimp Noodle Soup   33
Dim Sum Shrimp Dumplings with Three Dipping
Sauces   34
Marinated Asian Flank Steak   36
Cold Shrimp and Noodle Salad   37

6 The Most Perfect Meal Ever Made   38

The Basic Bird   39
The Spicy Bird   40
The Ultimate Bird   41
Gravy   42

7 The Perogie Ladies of Kamsack,
Saskatchewan   43

Perogie Dough with Three Fillings   44
The Best Ever Meat Loaf   46
Cabbage Bean Soup   46
Five-Minute Fudge   47
Poppy Seed Cake   48

8 The Wild Mushroom Hunt   49

Chicken Breasts Stuffed with Wild Mushrooms
and Porcini Butter   50
Wild Mushroom and Goat Cheese Omelette   52
Lamb Shanks with Root Veggies, Mushrooms,
and Gremolata   53

9 The Mighty Digby Scallop   55

Digby Scallop Mousse   57
Grilled Scallops with Sun-Dried Tomato Sauce   58

10 In Search of a Canadian Cuisine   59

Cinnamon Crust Breast of Turkey with Sweet and
    Spicy Thai Cream Sauce   60
Bar-b-qued Moose   61
Venison Shoulder Roast with Cranberry Cream
    Sauce   62
Roast Goose with Two Stuffings   63
Buffalo Eggplant Stew   65

11 Balsamico Traditionale   66

Balsamic Rhubarb Compote   67
New Potato, Goat Cheese, and Green Bean Salad with
    Sweet Balsamic Vinaigrette   68
Rosemary-Parmesan Mashed Potatoes   69
Calf's Liver with Bacon, Herbs, and Balsamic
    Vinegar   70
Corn and Tomatoes in Basil-Balsamic Butter   71

12 Really Great Canadian Wheat   72

Gnocchi alla Gorgonzola   73
Homemade Ravioli Stuffed with Roasted Squash and
    Goat Cheese in Frangelico Butter Sauce   74
Tagliatelle al Pollo   76
Penne with Sausages and Sun-Dried Tomatoes   77
Linguine with Clams, Tomatoes, and Arugula   78
Penne with Mushrooms and Proscuitto   79

13 Lunenburg Lobster   80

Roasted Lobster with Lemon Chive Oil   81
The Fabled Maritime Lobster Roll   82

14 Telderberry Wines   83

Baby Spinach and Mushroom Salad with Gorgonzola
    Cheese and Pears Poached in Strawberry Wine
    with Orange Vinaigrette   84
Maritime Oyster Chowder with Telderberry Apple
    Wine and Sweet Curried Whipped Cream   85
Filet of Atlantic Halibut Poached in Telderberry Pear
    Wine with Pear Wine Butter Sauce   87
Pan-Fried Medallions of Veal Striploin with
    Telderberry Blueberry Wine Reduction and Sage
    Oil   88

15 *Les Chefs des Chefs* and the Beaver
Club   90

Smoked Salmon and Arctic Char Tartare with Herb
    Sauce   91
Roast Loin of Caribou Lac St. Jean with Smoked Corn
    and Buckwheat Croquette and Berry Chutney in
    Blueberry Poivrade   92

16 The Queen's Chef   95

Grilled Breast of Chicken Filled with Oka Cheese
    and Fresh Sage   96
Bulgur Wheat and Wild Rice Risotto with Woodland
    Mushrooms   97
Sour Apricot Juice   99
Chocolate and Roasted Walnut Tart with Caramelized
    Peaches and Raspberry Sorbet   100

17 The Canadian VQA   101

Braised Short Ribs with Roasted Red Pepper and Red
    Wine Sauce   102
Pan-Roasted Potatoes   104
Pan-Wilted Garlic Spinach   104
Chicken Breasts in Riesling Sauce   105
Stuffed Veal Shoulder Roast in White Wine
    Reduction   106

18 The Culinary Grand Prix at
Whistler   108

Pork and Asparagus-Stuffed Parmesan
    Baskets   109
Chilled Smoked Salmon Soup with Chive Oil   110
Steak and Frites with Honey-Buttered
    Carrots   111
Pork Tenderloin in a Cassis Sauce   113
Beef and Pork Stew   114

19 The Pelican Grill and Kitchen Jim   116

Leek and Mussel Soup   117
P.E.I. Mussels with Cherry Tomatoes, Herbs, and
    Cream   118
Pelican Fuillette with Tarragon White Wine
    Sauce   119
Cherrywood-Grilled Arctic Char with Roasted
    Apple Coulis   121
Super-Fast Mussels with Garlic and Herbs   122
Mussels in Coconut and Lime Nectar   123
Key Lime Cheesecake Boisvert   124
Pecan Pumpkin Torte   125

20 Oyster Boy   127

Pan-Fried Oysters with Spicy Salsa   129
Skinny Oyster Po-Boy with Aioli and Chives   130
Bar-b-qued Oysters with Tequila Lime Butter   131

21 The Astorville Parish Picnic   132

Creamy Cold Cucumber and Bell Pepper
    Soup   133
Chicken and Veggie Salad with Lemon
    Vinaigrette   134
Curried Lamb and Sweet Potato Stew   135
Cipaille   136
Buttermilk Slaw   137
Three Bean Salad with Veggies   138

22 Recipes from the Columns   139

Shrimp Flambé with Proscuitto   140
Curried Squash Soup   141
Pan-Seared Breast of Duck in Soy-Honey
    Sauce   142
Cedar-Plank Salmon Marinated in Brandy and
    Earl Grey Tea   143
Chicken in Whisky Peanut Sauce   144
The Martooni Salad   145
Strawberries in Red Wine with Fresh Cracked
    Pepper   145
Peaches with Brandy   146

Index   147

Foreword

"You are what you eat." No truer words have ever been spoken. It is as true for your soul as it is for your bones. It is as relevant to your heritage as it is to your health. It is as meaningful to your own heart's desire as it is to the heart you desire. You are what you eat. And in Canada, we eat very well.

Food, and the selection and preparation thereof, is one of the two most fundamental instincts governing everyday life. Sex, specifically procreation and the resulting family, is the other. Food and sex. Eating and boinking. Survival in the immediate and the long run. These are primal lusts that inhabit, and occasionally inhibit, us all. Sorry, but in this book we only have time to go into the food. Besides, most of us get to eat three times a day, while sex on the other hand . . .

Welcome to *The Great Canadian Food Show*. Here you will find recipes, stories, adventures, and opinions culled from our travels and research in making season one of the television series we hope you know and love.

We are a merry band of food lovers who have had the distinct pleasure of travelling this continental country of ours in search of people who make their livings from one aspect or another of what we lovingly call "the Canadian food experience."

As cooking shows became all the rage, we decided to do a show about eating: Let's travel from one end of the country to the other and do stories about Canadians who love food. Let's do stories about the best in the land, about passion, about love, and, above all, about really great food! And while we were at it, we decided to shoot all our stories in both French and English...something that had never been done before in the history of Canadian television. So we put together a team of the best camera operators (hereafter known as "shooters"), sound guys (hereafter known as "sound guys"), and directors (hereafter known as "les grand fromages"), and set out to discover Canada.

Our hosts for this adventure were Carlo Rota, Esquire, a naturalized Canadian of Italian descent who speaks with an English accent, and Natalie Richard, a multi-talented goddess from downtown Montreal...both of whom are perfect for a show about Canada! Both hosts had extensive food backgrounds (Carlo's dad ran many well-known restaurants in Torontosaurus Rex, including Noodles and Da Dante, while the urbane Nat was raised on an organic apple farm outside Quebec City) and could speak about the topic at hand with passion and credibility.

We are citizens of a country that can geographically accommodate continental Europe with room to spare. If the United States is the great melting pot, then surely Canada is the great buffet...all you can eat, never the same meal twice!

We are a country of bountiful harvest and a breath-taking array of foodstuff. Canada has brought together the best of all the nations of the world. In Canada we are afforded unprecedented support and supply to be ourselves and to contribute to a wonderful free collective, without giving up that from whence we came. No matter your god or country, your past or your pasta, your heritage or your age, all are welcome in this benevolent society. We are a nation of people who have come looking for something better, and despite being buried under a fathom of snow half the year we have all found it here in Canada. As you can tell, we're kinda juiced on Canada.

As "foodies," we are particularly ecstatic about the plenitude of world cuisines that are now considered "Canadian." Is jerk chicken any less ours than the prairie wheat brought here by an earlier wave of immigrants? Virtually every nation of the world has a son or daughter who now calls Canada home. With them they have brought their customs and cuisines, for which we are all grateful. Imagine someone's first winter in Winnipeg after a life in Vietnam...how strange this place must have seemed at first. On the other hand, consider the first Scottish settlers who, upon first sighting Cape Breton Island, could be forgiven for thinking they had somehow gotten turned around in the night and were looking at bonnie Scotland!

We Canucks have it all: the best beef, the best pork, the best fruit and veggies, incredible dairy...you get the idea. Nowhere else in the world will you find such an amazing diversity of foodstuff grown, raised, packaged, marketed, cooked, preserved, and eaten. Rejoice, friends, in the wonderful diversity and richness of this country we call home. Do not go gently into that good night, but rather order up a large thin crust with extra cheese, or place your soul squarely in your walking shoes and frequent a restaurant whose name you can't pronounce. Come over to the bright side. Let your taste buds be your conscience, let your tummy be your compass, and explore the world as it unfolds before you in your pantry, your grocer, your local market, your sense of adventure.

We live in an age where we are told that shopping and cooking and eating and spending time in the kitchen is a waste. Those money traders in the temple of your good taste are wrong: Food is not dead; it's alive and glorious and most definitely not microwaveable or found at a drive-through window. Good food is the very soul of your existence. You are what you eat. Don't give in to those who would tell you that a meal is a necessary evil, something to be scarfed down as quickly as possible, so that you can get on with other things. After all, my God, is there any other occasion that is as meaningful to family and loved ones as sitting around even the simplest dinner table and sharing...and caring...and communicating...and being family. Think about it: Every meaningful event in your life has involved food in some way. If you're a religious person, your temple of worship undoubtedly has at least one ritual that involves eating or drinking. On a more secular note, how about that first date with the one you love? Chances are you went out for something to eat. Not to mention your wedding, your funeral, your wake. All great events in your life have to do with eating. All meaningless events in your life have to do with eating...hey, you gotta chow down three square meals or else – and the "else" is your health and well-being. Sooner or later, it all comes back to how and what you eat. Don't give in to those who would tell you that food and cooking and eating is an inconvenience to be done away with as quickly as possible. Don't buy crap-in-a-can. Don't be intimidated by what should be the most

natural and enjoyable thing in your whole life (except for sneezing...pound for pound, there's nothing quite as enjoyable as sneezing). You are most definitely what you eat. This is not only true of your sinew and bone marrow and fibrillation and blood flow but also of your soul...and your passion...and your joie de vivre...and your lust...and all those things that make you special and different and worthwhile yet do not register on a thermometer or X-ray or CAT scan. You know what we're talking about! Food and cooking unleashes the passion in you. It gives you a reason to live. It is Viagra for the soul. Eat well, friend. It's the best thing we could ever wish for you.

We would be remiss if we did not take a minute to thank everyone who made this book, and indeed the television series itself, possible. By our count, over 100 people have either worked on or been featured in the show and this book. That's a lot of beautiful caring folk who are as passionate about food and Canada as we are.

Now, get yourself a big glass of good Canadian wine, kick back, and give us a read. We hope you enjoy our humble offering. *Salut!*

Introduction

Things You Absolutely Positively Have to Know Before Reading This Book or Attempting Any of the Recipes

Buy Fresh, Buy Local, Buy Canadian

We heard an interview once about how important it was to take your kids out to the country and show them where food really comes from. After all, to a four-year-old all food comes from the supermarket and is canned, frozen, boxed, or wrapped in cellophane. A child does not naturally make the leap that all the food we consume was once a living, growing thing, be it animal or vegetable. We think it's important that all of us, adult and child, get to know where our food comes from and who grows it. What's more, you can't go wrong supporting local suppliers and farmers. Your neighbour deserves your support and will repay you and your family with good, fresh, local food for years to come. If local isn't available, at least buy Canadian whenever possible. In the wine business there is the term *gout du terroir*, which quite literally means "taste of the terrain" or "taste of the earth." It refers to the nutrients drawn up from the soil by the grape that gives it a taste different from the wine made in the next valley or country. Just as the grape is a sponge, soaking up the goodness from the earth, so are asparagus and cattle and fish and tomatoes. Canada has great soil, ipso facto Canada has great food. It's that simple. Our stuff is as good or better than that anywhere else in the world. Buy Canadian.

Special Equipment Needed to Prepare These Recipes

We have modified recipes from the great kitchens of Canada to accommodate the equipment and space found in your typical home. The only items some people might not have are:

A candy thermometer: Also known as a cooking thermometer. It only costs a couple of bucks and you'll need it to make caramel sauce and when deep-frying. Some folks use it to determine whether a piece of meat is properly cooked.

A hand mixer: Possibly the single greatest invention since the oven itself. A hand mixer saves times in puréeing soups and sauces and has none of the mess you get using a blender. You can buy a good one with some neat attachments for chopping and dicing for around $25. It's the one "time-saving" kitchen tool that really delivers.

A splash guard: Sits on top of your saucepan or skillet as liquids bubble away. It has a fine mesh cover so you can see what is going on in the pot but your stove-top doesn't get dirty from the liquids percolating. There are many recipes that involve the wonderful magic of sauce reduction or deep-frying or soup making, and this is one handy little item that will save you lots of clean-up time.

Cooking twine: Also known as kitchen string and essential for tying up stuffed roasts, turkeys, and naughty sous-chefs.

Cooking Techniques

Obviously we would like this book to be of use to as many people as possible, and we are mindful that readers will have varying degrees of cooking skills. Some of the techniques you'll need to know for this book include clarifying butter, making stocks, making a brown sauce, oven-roasting nuts, peeling mangoes, and making croutons. If you are already practised in these skills, all the better. If you are not, please, please, please don't be put off or intimidated. Remember that cooking and eating are adventures and should, by nature, expose you to new and wonderful things. Don't be afraid to mess up. Even the best chefs in the world make a muck of things from time to time. There is any number of wonderful books available that explain the basics for you. Our favourite is the old tried and tested *New York Times Cookbook*, which includes a gazillion great recipes and all the cooking techniques you'll ever need to know.

We Made Every Single Recipe Ourselves!

It is standard procedure for cookbook authors to use professional test kitchens and food economists in developing the recipes contained in their books. We did not do that. We made every single one of the recipes in this book at home ourselves. Why? It's simple: How could we possibly expect you to make the recipes at home if we can't do them ourselves? Every single recipe has been made in our not-so-state-of-the-art kitchens staffed by untrained, eager, and hungry foodies. Remember: We're not professional chefs; we're just a bunch of food-lovin' schmoes who count our lucky stars that we have had the opportunity to do this show and write this book. Cooking can be practised with satisfaction and joy at many levels of proficiency. All it takes is a little enthusiasm and knowing that it ain't no biggie if you screw up a recipe.

To ensure that the recipes contained herein are not too difficult or over the top, we've experimented on friends. Long-time bachelor executroids with Chinese takeout and pizza on their speed dials have made the steak and frites, leek and mussel soup, halibut poached in pear wine, and Vietnamese beef and shrimp noodle soup featured in this book (we selected the recipes at random). If these guys can cook, anybody can!

The Importance of Presentation

It has long been held in Japanese cuisine that first one eats with one's eyes. Hence your typical plate of Japanese sashimi looks like a work of art. We are of the same mind. At the end of most recipes you will find serving and plating suggestions. Take them, use them, throw them away, and try new things yourself. Remember: The presentation of the food one cooks is directly proportional to the pride one takes in having cooked it. Your biggest wow is going to come in that moment when the plate hits the table and your guests are teased by the aromas that waft up at them and seduced by the way you arrange your creation on your stoneware canvas.

Read the Recipes from Start to End and Then Improvise

It is important to read every recipe through once (this applies to all recipes, not just the ones in this book) and then sit down for a moment and visualize yourself making it. No joke . . . professional athletes and performance artists do it all the time. See yourself making the stock or braising the tenderloin . . . have the meal finished in your mind before you even begin making it. Then follow your heart. With the exception of most baking recipes, which require exact timing and specific quantities of ingredients, all others should be signposts on your culinary journey . . . personalize your creation, add more or less garlic, throw in some Pernod or a bay leaf if you are so moved. The important thing is to have fun and experiment in the kitchen. No meal crafted with love and enthusiasm has ever failed to please. Have fun!

The greatest self-indulgence: A butane torch.
These handy dandy kitchen torches do more than make the perfect crème brûlée. We use ours to finish off mashed potatoes, shrimp, tenderloins, bread, and veggie stacks, giving them all a wonderful charred outer texture.

The worst kitchen appliance/gadget ever invented: The microwave.
Microwave ovens are great for defrosting frozen food, melting chocolate or butter, heating liquids, or zapping an undercooked bit of meat. Beyond these remedial time-saving functions, a microwave has no use or place in your kitchen. It is an abomination visited upon us by those people who insist that cooking is a chore, to be done away with as quickly as possible, regardless of taste. To cook with a microwave is to prepare food minus the most important ingredient you have to offer...your soul. It is passionless food heated over, atoms and molecules agitated and not nurtured. No good can come from a microwave, dear reader; do not go over to the dark side; resist the temptation. But all is not lost! There is a new generation of ovens on the way that combines microwave technology and conventional ovens...a development we look forward to playing with!

The greatest waste of time: The electric can opener.
Never did understand this one. It actually takes longer to open a can with an electric opener than with a manual opener. You don't save any time and, let's face it, opening a can isn't exactly slave labour!

Heli-Hiking and the Canadian Bar-b-que

*"The wonderful world of home appliances now make it possible
to cook indoors with charcoal and outdoors with gas..."*
Bill Vaughan

Three things mark the advent of warm weather in Canada — hockey playoffs, red robins, and the unmistakable aroma of backyard bar-b-ques fired up for another season of outdoor grilling.

We knew that we had to do a mondo bar-b-que story for *The Great Canadian Food Show*...it's such a big beautiful country out there, though, that we couldn't figure out where to do the story. Is a bar-b-que any better in Lethbridge than in St. John's? While researching the story we tried to figure out what goes into making a great bar-b-que. We knew it was one cooking experience everyone could relate to regardless of culinary prowess, and we wanted to give it a twist with great visuals. In fact, "The World's Greatest Bar-b-que" was the first episode we shot for the series, so it had to be pretty special.

We finally decided on a bar-b-que way up in the Rockies, for two reasons: one, it don't get much prettier than that and, two, we all wanted to ride in helicopters. After a seven-hour drive from Calgary (the last hour of which was on a bumpy mountain logging road barely wide enough for one vehicle and designed to set your back teeth floating) we reached the Bobby Burns Lodge, run by Canadian Mountain Holidays and smack dab in the middle of the Bugaboos.

Canadian Mountain Holidays (CMH) was started in 1957 by a young Austrian immigrant named Hans Gmoser. It is a funky cutting-edge operation that runs a heli-skiing operation in the winter covering some 10,000 square kilometres of virgin mountain vertical for the long-ski trucker. In the summer, CMH offers the same chopper experience with guided hiking tours and serious mountain climbing. The terrain provides extreme rappelling off cliff faces, brisk hikes through mountain passes, and leisurely strolls in stunning mountain glades.

CMH is a turnkey operation with six luxurious lodges spread across the mountain range. They've got boots, jackets, walking poles, backpacks, friendly and experienced guides who genuinely love the mountains, and, of course, the really cool helicopters. Heli-hikers come in all ages and sizes. We were there on the Tuesday following Labour Day and joined a mixed group of about 20 hardy hikers from all over Canada, the United States, and Europe.

Choppering up to a mountain glade is an indescribable experience, as you pass over ground never trod on by human foot. Consider your place in the universe while you contemplate the egress of an ancient glacier. The guides at CMH will custom-design the hike to your fitness level and interests. Walking throught the Bugaboos is as close as most of us will ever come to the top of the world. The air is as crisp as peppermint and the scenery is in brilliant, sharp focus. There is a peace and tranquility that comes from being up there that you won't find anywhere else. It's also a great way to work up an appetite!

Sitting on a rock at 7000 feet looking out over a glacier while munching on a bison burger is a very satisfying moment. The chipmunks up there are called ground squirrels and are about the size of a large dog. At least two or three times a year, an unwitting hiker will be ambushed by several ground squirrels working as a pack and carried off to work in a secret ground squirrel diamond mine. Most heli-hiking choppers are equipped with ground squirrel–seeking missiles called "squirreler whirlers." Once, we also thought we'd seen the elusive sasquatch rumoured to live in those parts. As it turned out, it was only our director, Trevor Grant, having a bad hair day. Seriously though, a day traipsing around the Bugaboos is guaranteed to bring you one of the best night's sleep of your life! After carbing up on a delicious big dinner and drinking a relaxing cognac by the fire, it's time to retire to your room and drift off into la-la land under a soft down-filled duvet. It ain't cheap, but it is a wonderful experience well worth looking into.

The bar-b-que we did on that show was a simple one that emphasized fresh local ingredients, namely bison burgers, grilled free-range chicken, venison bratwurst, veggie burgers, lots of salads, fresh local trout cooked in foil, and mint ice tea.

In this episode, we hope we captured the joy and fun of a bar-b-que rather than specific recipes. Obviously bison burgers and venison bratwurst are not readily available at your local grocers. What follows are some of *our* favorite bar-b-que recipes we've picked up in our travels. The couscous recipe is of course from the heli-hiking episode.

Grilled Leg of Lamb

2/3 cup	olive oil	150 ml
1/2 cup + 2 tbsp	big dry red wine with legs	125 ml + 30 ml
1/4 cup	red wine vinegar	50 ml
2 tbsp	good-quality balsamic vinegar	30 ml
1/3 cup	fresh diced rosemary	75 ml
10	garlic cloves, pressed	10
5 lb	leg of lamb, butterflied with bone removed	2.5 kg
	Salt and freshly cracked pepper	

1 Mix all the marinade ingredients in a big glass bowl and add the lamb. Turn several times with your hands to make sure that all of the lamb is covered. Cover with tin foil and refrigerate for at least 24 hours, turning every now and then. Remove from the fridge about an hour before grilling so as to return lamb to room temperature.

2 Remove lamb from marinade and sprinkle generously with salt and fresh cracked pepper.

3 Grill the lamb on the centre of the bar-b-que for about 17 minutes over medium heat for medium rare, or for 23 minutes for medium. Don't worry about the flare-ups, as these will give you a delicious crispy skin. Turn the meat only once and cook for another 17 to 23 minutes, depending on how you like your lamb cooked.

4 Remove lamb from grill and tent with tin foil for 20 minutes to allow juices to settle. Carve slices and serve.

This is another incredibly simple recipe that provides incredible results. Lamb is one of the most fantabulous meats you could ever linger over with friends and a big bottle of red wine. It is best served with the couscous that Carlo helped make in this episode (recipe follows).

Please, please, please do not serve mint jelly with this fantastic cut of meat. The rosemary and garlic have infused the lamb during the marinating. Trust us. With any luck, there will be some lamb remaining for the greatest leftover sandwich ever – thinly sliced cold lamb on sourdough bread with unsalted butter, hot mustard, salt, and fresh pepper!

Serves 6

6 tips for better bar-b-queing

☾ Don't overcrowd the grill, as it slows down the cooking and gives you dried-out meat. Leave a good 3/4 inch (2 cm) between pieces.

✤ Pat your meat (or chicken or fish) dry before grilling, then add whatever spices you desire.

↔ Throw some dried oregano, basil, or sage on the charcoal or lava rocks just before grilling for a nice "smoking" effect.

▽ Make sure everything is at room temperature before grilling. Cold meats and cold basting sauces slow down the cooking process.

✤ If you're watching your cholesterol, remove the skin from chicken after grilling, as the skin holds in the natural moisture of the bird.

⃠ Never marinate in a metal bowl. Most marinades include an acidic ingredient like vinegar or wine that breaks down the toughness of a piece of meat and that reacts badly with metal and can ruin the taste of dinner.

Grilled Asparagus and Pork Salad

This is also a great meal on its own and a nice change from burgers and dogs. Feel free to experiment with the vinaigrette. If you can't find the thick-stalked asparagus, go for the thin guys but don't halve them. Mesclun can sometimes be on the expensive side, so a good substitute is fresh baby spinach leaves.

Serves 6 as an appetizer

1/4 cup	hoisin sauce*	50 ml
1/4 cup	white vinegar	50 ml
1/4 cup	chicken or vegetable broth (preferably low-salt)	50 ml
3 tbsp	diced fresh garlic	45 ml
2 tbsp	soy sauce	30 ml
1 tsp	sweet mustard**	5 ml
1 tsp	bottled horseradish**	5 ml
Approximately 1 1/2 lb	fresh asparagus, thick stalks only	700 g
Approximately 1 lb	pork tenderloin	500 g
2 tbsp	freshly cracked pepper	30 ml
2 tsp	freshly ground coriander seeds	10 ml
2 tsp	freshly ground fennel seeds	10 ml
	Mesclun (fancy-shmancy mixed greens)	

* *Hoisin sauce (also known as Peking sauce) is made from soybean, garlic, chili peppers, and a bunch of spices. It is absolutely delicious and is available in Asian grocery stores and some of your better mainstream supermarkets. Once you have some in your fridge, you'll wonder how you ever got by without it.*

** *You can substitute 1 tbsp (15 ml) of Dijon mustard if you don't have these ingredients handy.*

1 Blend the first 7 ingredients in a mixer or food processor until smooth.

2 Cut the asparagus stalks lengthwise and soak them in cold water for at least half an hour.

3 Get the bar-b-que to medium high.

4 Pat the tenderloin dry and cut a ¼-inch-deep incision running lengthwise to even out the thickness.

5 Rub the tenderloin on all sides with the peppercorns, coriander, and fennel. Now you have a nice spicy coating that is going to form a wonderful crust on the que without drying the meat.

6 Grill the tenderloin for about 5 minutes on each side until just done. Remove from the grill and tent with foil to keep warm.

7 Grill the asparagus cut-side-down, then turn after 2 minutes or when you see the asparagus begin to char. It will also turn a wonderful bright green as the increased water content begins to steam out. Remove asparagus from grill when done.

8 Cut the tenderloin crosswise into long thin slices.

9 Place pork slices and asparagus on a bed of mixed greens and drizzle with the vinaigrette.

Bar-b-qued Sardines

12	fresh sardines, heads removed, cleaned and gutted	12
1/2 cup	olive oil (for grilling)	125 ml
	Salt and freshly cracked pepper	
3 tbsp	finely chopped fresh oregano	45 ml
1	zucchini, peel on, finely chopped	1
1/2	red pepper, seeds removed and diced	1/2
1/2	yellow pepper, seeds removed and diced	1/2
1	carrot, peeled and diced	1
3	shallots, finely diced	3
4 tbsp	bottled Italian dressing (use low-cal if you like)	60 ml

1 Set your bar-b-que on medium-high.
2 Rinse the sardines under cold water. Pat the outsides dry with paper towel, butterfly them, and place skin-side-down on a baking sheet. Pat the meat side dry as well. Brush the fish with the olive oil and season with salt and fresh cracked pepper. Sprinkle the oregano over the fish.
3 Combine the zucchini, red and yellow peppers, carrot, and shallots in a bowl. Add the Italian dressing and season with salt and fresh cracked pepper. Cover with plastic wrap and set aside at room temperature.
4 Brush the remaining olive oil onto your grill and bar-b-que the sardines for about 2 minutes a side or until crispy golden brown.
5 Place two sardines, skin side down, on each serving plate and top with a spoonful of the vegetable mixture. Serve immediately with grilled zucchini slices and lemon wedges, because there is nothing worse than a cold sardine (isn't there a song about that?).

Unless your family has roots in the Mediterranean, chances are you have never enjoyed the wonderful experience of a fresh sardine. Like tuna and salmon, a fresh sardine bears little resemblance, in taste or texture, to the canned version. The flesh is tender and sweet with a taste considerably more delicate than the packed-in-oil fillets. Sardine is not so much a fish per se as it is a variety, referring to any number of small silver-skinned fish. Your local fishmonger will usually get them in the summertime. Ask him to gut, clean, and remove the heads for you. This is a wonderfully simple appetizer for your next bar-b-que.

Serves 6 as an appetizer

Lemon Grilled Zucchini

This is a super-simple recipe. The lemon juice marinade infuses the zucchini with a wonderful citrus bite. Serve the zuke with grilled red and yellow pepper slices. All the vitamins are in the skin, so don't peel it unless you have to.

Serves 6

3	large zucchini, cut in half and then halved again, (or 6 small ones, halved)	3
	Juice of 2 lemons	
2 tbsp	olive oil	30 ml
	Fresh cracked pepper to taste	

1 Combine all the ingredients in a glass bowl and marinate for at least half an hour.
2 Grill the zucchini flat side down first, for about 3 to 4 minutes on a medium-high grill till you get nice deep brown grill marks on the white flesh of the zucchini.
3 Turn the zucchini once and continue to grill for 2 minutes.
4 Serve very hot or the zucchini will go limp and lose its oomph.

Bugaboo Couscous

Couscous (not to be confused with *coush-coush*, which is a gooey cornmeal-based Cajun breakfast sludge also good for plastering walls in a pinch) hails originally from North Africa and is readily available in most supermarkets. Basically, it is semolina (Durham wheat) and is very simple to prepare. It's a nice change from potatoes or rice as the starch component in a meal. These teeny-tiny pasta balls (a lot of people think they're actually a grain like micro-rice but in fact they're really pasta) can be served hot or cold and are ready in minutes.

Serves 6

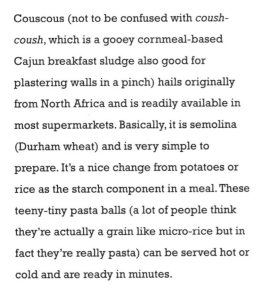

1 1/2 cups	chicken stock	375 ml
2 cups	couscous	500 ml
1/2 cup	chopped green onion	125 ml
1 cup	thinly sliced fresh basil	250 ml
	Juice of 1 lemon	
1 tsp	grated lemon peel	5 ml
	Freshly cracked pepper	

1 Bring the broth to a boil in a large saucepan.
2 Add the couscous and stir.
3 Remove saucepan from heat, cover, and let stand for about 10 minutes.
4 Fold in all other ingredients.

Can be served warm or at room temperature, or cold with leftovers.

Bar-b-qued Pineapple

1	large pineapple, skin removed but core intact	1
8	whole cloves	8
3/4 cup	pure maple syrup	175 ml

1 Stick the cloves into various parts of the pineapple flesh.
2 Put the pineapple and the maple syrup into a large sealable baggie and marinate in the fridge overnight. Remove from the fridge an hour before cooking to return to room temperature.
3 Heat bar-b-que to medium.
4 If you have a rotisserie, skewer the pineapple through the middle and roast, covered, for about 30 minutes, basting with leftover syrup. If you do not have a rotisserie, cut the pineapple into 12 slices and grill for about 3 minutes per side, turning only once.
5 Serve with really top-drawer vanilla ice cream or with whipped cream and a sugar biscuit.

We know that pineapples aren't Canadian (although Sooke Harbour House on Vancouver Island does grow a variety of pineapple in their wonderful gardens, but the maple syrup is. This is an easy, elegant dessert that will blow everyone away. Don't forget to clean the grill first!

Serves 6

The Quebec City Bistros

2

Get thee to old Quebec City, for it is possibly the most beautiful city in all of the Dominion. It is certainly the most romantic, and should never ever be visited without someone special nuzzled on your arm. As Carlo says, "To walk these streets alone, to visit these restaurants . . . is to drink fine wine from a paper cup. A sorry tale indeed!" To walk through the big stone gates into the old city is to step onto the narrow cobblestone streets of Lyons or Avignon or Paris (only you don't have to put up with snooty waiters and outrageous prices). *"La vieille ville"* has an old-world charm you will not find anywhere else in North America (old Montreal is close). It is Disneyland for the gourmet and Vegas for the romantic. Best of all, Quebec City wears its big generous heart proudly on its sleeve. The people there are genuinely friendly and quite content to live in a beautiful place

busting at the seams with *"el touristos."* Unfortunately, the same cannot be said of Paris, which, while being a beautiful city, is full of hoity-toity Parisians.

There is a half-a-klik stretch just outside the gates, called *La Grande Allee,* reminiscent of the main boulevard in Aix-en-Provence in the south of France. In these few blocks are 20-odd bars and bistros in old converted greystone walk-ups set back from the street. Many have rows of small tables facing onto the street (à la français) facilitating a leisurely afternoon of people watching. A leisurely couple of hours sitting next to your honey watching the world go by. This practice is all-too-uncommon in Canada. How unfortunate for us.

And, man, do these people love to eat! There are fabulous restaurants to fit any budget scattered throughout the city, and lots of well-stocked charcuteries, aromatic *boulangeries,* and mouth-watering patisseries.

You cannot help but eat well. Quebec City runs on its tummy. Avoid the bus-tour joints and explore the backstreets…smack your heels on the cobblestones and stroll till you find that perfect little boîte.

The entire "Quebec City Bistro" episode was shot in both languages over the course of one and a half very long days. First we'd shoot a scene in French with Carlo as Natalie's guest, then we'd stop, reset, relight, and reshoot the same scene in English with the roles reversed. We had two camera crews who would hopscotch each other around the city. The Quebec City tourism people were A-1 when racing us around town and loading and unloading gear, not quite sure what we were doing but always accommodating. While one crew set up, the other was shooting. Then we'd rush Carlo and Natalie on to the next location. We were intense and harried and quite obtrusive, but absolutely everyone was friendly and patiently put up with the cameras and lights and multiple takes and close ups and . . . well, you get the idea. Our shortest day was 19 hours of continual shooting, striking, setting, shooting, setting . . . at the end of it all we were dead on our feet but happy with the footage we had captured.

Anyway, if you have a romantic bone in your body, do yourself a favour and take your best gal or your best guy to *la ville de Québec*.

Here are a few recipes inspired by the restaurants we had the pleasure of visiting . . .

Recipes from Le Café du Monde

Le Café du Monde is a *très*-chic bistro in the heart of the old city that has a funky, sophisticated air about it. The tunes are great, the clientele is hip, and the wine list is long and reasonable. When you order the grape, a bottle is placed on your table and you pay for whatever you consume. Regulars write their names on the bottle and it is kept in the cellar for them so they can finish it off over two or three visits. A very accommodating practice more restaurants might want to adopt. Le Café du Monde features classic French bistro food, and they do it very well. We chose two very different dishes to feature: an uncooked tartare and a slow-cooked confit bubbled in its own fat . . . mmmm! These recipes are as far apart on the cooking Richter scale as you can get and represent the diversity of options available when you start with good fresh ingredients. It ain't gotta be complicated to be tasty!

Tartare aux Deux Saumons

Once you've tried this recipe, do some experimenting of your own by adding Dijon mustard, finely diced garlic and parsley, finely diced pickle, Asian garlic chili sauce, or lime juice.

When preparing raw salmon, it is important to always use the freshest ingredients possible. Tell your fishmonger that you intend to use the salmon raw so that he gives you sushi-grade fillets. Buy the salmon no more than a few hours before using and keep it in the fridge. Remember: The Japanese have been eating raw fish for a few thousand years and are doing quite well, thank you very much. Just use a little common sense and enjoy the taste unavailable from any fish once tempered by flame.

The same thing applies to the raw egg yolks. Make sure they're as fresh as possible. Yo, people! This is Canada! We have the best, the freshest, the safest food on the planet. Revel in it...eat it up...embrace it!

Serves 6 as an appetizer

3/4 lb	fresh salmon fillets, skin removed	350 g
3/4 lb	smoked salmon	350 g
5	egg yolks	5
	Juice of 1 lemon	
3 tbsp	finely diced white or red onion	45 ml
3 tbsp	diced capers	45 ml
1 tbsp	finely diced chives	15 ml
10	dashes Worcestershire sauce	10
6	dashes Tabasco sauce	6

1 Cut both salmons into strips.
2 Mix the salmon with all the other ingredients in a bowl.
3 Season to taste with salt and fresh cracked pepper.
4 Serve on a bed of greens or on a single kale leaf with toasted baguette slices.

Confit de Canard, Pommes à l'Ail

	Sea salt	
10	bay leaves, crumbled	10
1	bunch thyme, roughly chopped	1
12	medium-sized duck legs	12
2 quarts	rendered duck fat	2 L
6	large russet potatoes	6
	Salt and freshly cracked pepper	
2 tbsp	diced garlic	30 ml
2 tbsp	diced fresh parsley	30 ml

This is possibly the most delicious dish in the history of French cuisine. You can buy rendered duck fat (which has a very high smoking point and lots of taste) and duck legs at better butchers in your home town. This is a special-occasion meal and takes a while to prepare, but trust us, it's worth the effort.

Serves 6 as a main course

The night before the dinner:

1 Mix the sea salt, bay leaves, and thyme in a small bowl.

2 Rub the duck legs with the mixture, place them in a shallow dish, cover tightly with plastic wrap, and put in the fridge overnight.

The next morning:

1 Heat the duck fat in a large casserole over medium-high heat.

2 Wipe the duck legs clean of the dry rub.

3 Place the duck legs into the fat once it is very hot and let them bubble away for about 25 minutes or until they are golden brown.

4 Reduce heat to medium-low and continue simmering for 1 hour.

5 Remove casserole from heat, cover, and put to one side.

At dinnertime:

1 Peel, wash, and cut potatoes into half-inch squares or rounds.

2 Place the potatoes in a pot of cold water and bring to a boil.

3 Blanch the potatoes for about 4 minutes, strain, and refresh by running under cold water.

4 Remove ½ cup (125 ml) of duck fat from the casserole and put in a large skillet over medium heat. Return casserole to burner and reheat on medium.

5 Add the potatoes to the skillet and cook until golden brown, mixing occasionally. Season with salt and fresh cracked pepper.

6 Add garlic and parsley to the potatoes, reduce heat to low, and sauté for 30 seconds.

7 Using tongs, plate two duck legs and potatoes for each guest, garnish with fresh thyme, and serve with a big salad of mixed greens with a simple balsamic dressing.

Recipes from Graffitti

While Quebec City is known for its French cuisine, it also has lots of great Italian restaurants, and Graffitti is one of the best. Okay, so technically Graffitti is not in the old city. But it is not far outside the old stone walls and is a calming, urbane kind of place that looks out onto rue Cartier. Ask for a seat in the outer atrium. Go for dinner and you'll likely find owners Adolpho and Mario Bernardo working the floor, making sure everything is just so. Get Adolpho to give you a tour of their award-winning wine cellar in the basement. Whatever you do, don't leave without having dessert! Here, then, is our take on some classic Italian dishes as inspired by the culinary talents of the brothers Bernardo.

Most Excellent Fish Soup

In Italian this dish is called *"zuppa di pesce."* Sounds a lot more delectable, doesn't it? Ah, those crafty Italians have a different word for everything! The French, specifically they of Marseilles, lay claim to the ultimate fish soup, namely bouillabaisse. However, the Italians and Greeks and all the other countries bordering on the Mediterranean also have wonderful seafood potions worthy of consideration, not to mention such heavenly creations as sen-chung-shea-gai, a peppery hot fish soup from Japan. We have quantified this one as a main course. Serve it with lots of crusty bread and a lovely lima bean salad (recipe follows). For dessert, serve apples with cinnamon Calvados cream (recipe follows). Don't be put off by the number of ingredients, as this is a one-pot meal that cooks itself.

Serves 6 as a main course

2/3 lb	large shrimp (about 12), peeled and deveined	300 g
2/3 lb	Canadian sea scallops	300 g
	Salt and freshly cracked pepper	
4 tbsp	unsalted butter	60 ml
1 tbsp	olive oil	15 ml
2	medium leeks, white part only, washed and coarsely chopped	2
3	garlic cloves, finely diced	3
1/2 tsp	saffron	2 ml
	Dried hot pepper flakes, to taste	
1 tsp	dried oregano	5 ml
1 tsp	dried thyme	5 ml
1 cup	white wine	250 ml
3 tbsp	cognac	45 ml
24	small clams, scrubbed	24
24	mussels, scrubbed	24
4	bottles of clam juice (about 3 cups/750 ml)	4
	Juice of 1 lemon	
8	plum tomatoes, seeded and coarsely chopped	8
1 1/2 lb	meaty white fish fillets (such as sea bass), cut into bite-size pieces	700 g
6 tbsp	coarsely chopped fresh basil	90 ml
6 tbsp	coarsely chopped fresh parsley	90 ml

1 Pat the shrimp and scallops dry with paper towel and season with salt and fresh cracked pepper. Add the butter and olive oil to a

medium soup pot over a medium-high heat. Wait until the butter begins to foam and add the shrimp and scallops. Let them cook for about 1 minute per side, or until they've browned. Do not turn the scallops over more than once and don't worry if they're not cooked through, as you'll finish them off later in the soup. Transfer the shrimp and scallops to a bowl and set aside.

2 Add the leeks, garlic, saffron, hot pepper flakes, and herbs to the pot and sauté for 1 minute, stirring constantly. Add the white wine and cognac and bring to a boil.

3 Add the clams and cover the pot. Cook for 3 minutes. Add the mussels and stir well. Put the lid back on and cook for another 5 minutes. Just imagine the aroma that is going to hit you at this moment . . . the wine and garlic and herbs and saffron and seafood-ieness all bubbling away, creating this intense amber liquid! Yum!

4 Pour in the clam juice, lemon juice, and tomatoes and bring to a boil. Add the shrimp, scallops, and fish pieces to the pot and cover for another 3 minutes. Remove the pot from the heat and add the basil and parsley. Mix well.

5 To serve, divide the shrimp, scallops, and fish pieces between 6 large serving bowls and top with ladlefuls of the broth. Be sure to throw out any scallops or mussels that did not open.

SOUTH

Lima Bean Salad

Approximately 1 lb	lima beans	500 g
	(if using frozen, make sure	
	they're completely thawed)	
1	red bell pepper, roasted and cut	1
	into long strips	
1	yellow bell pepper, roasted and	1
	cut into long strips	
2	plum tomatoes, seeded and diced	2
1	zucchini, peeled and diced	1
4 tbsp	diced fennel tops	60 ml
	Salt and freshly cracked pepper, to taste	
1/3 cup	olive oil	75 ml
	Juice of 1 lemon	
1/4 tsp	dried oregano	1 ml
20	fresh basil leaves, washed	20
1 1/4 cup	croutons	300 ml

The Italians love their lima beans and we don't eat enough of them here. Lima beans look like kidney beans but are a lovely pale yellowy-green in colour. South of the Mason–Dixon line they're called butter beans. If you can't get fresh, go for frozen, but stay away from the canned variety. In this recipe we match the beans with sweet bell peppers and crunchy fennel, another wonderful ingredient that doesn't get enough of a showing here in the colonies.

Serves 6 as a side plate with the fish soup or as a starter on its own

1 Combine the lima beans, red and yellow peppers, tomatoes, zucchini, and fennel tops in a large bowl. Season with salt and fresh cracked pepper and toss.

2 Whisk the olive oil, lemon juice, and oregano together to make a dressing. Pour the dressing over the lima bean mixture and toss. Add the basil and croutons to the bowl and toss again. Serve immediately, before the croutons get soggy.

Apples with Cinnamon Calvados Cream

Is this meal easy or what? The fish soup is done in one pot, the lima bean salad takes no time to throw together, and you can steam these delicious apples while everyone is resting after the main course. Presto, pronto, bingo! Good food doesn't have to be complicated. Calvados is an exceptional apple-based brandy from Normandy in northern France. If you don't want to pop for an entire bottle, we've tried this recipe with the same quantity of Grand Marnier with excellent results, and you can buy Grand Marnier in the single-serving bottles if you don't have any on hand.

Serves 6 as a dessert

1/2 cup	raisins or dried cranberries	125 ml
3/4 cup	Calvados	175 ml
6 tbsp	crumbled graham crackers	90 ml
1/3 cup	almonds, chopped	75 ml
1/3 cup	pine nuts, chopped	75 ml
1/3 cup	walnuts, chopped	75 ml
6	crispy ripe sweet apples	6
1 cup	35% cream	250 ml
3 tbsp	ground cinnamon	45 ml

1 Soak the raisins (or cranberries) in the Calvados for 30 minutes.

2 Strain the Calvados and reserve. Combine the raisins, graham crackers, almonds, pine nuts, and walnuts in a bowl and mix well.

3 Cut the tops off the apples and set aside. Scoop out a good two-thirds of the apple. Discard the core and add the apple chunks to the raisin and nut mixture. Pour in 3 tbsp (45 ml) of the Calvados and mix well. Make sure the apple chunks aren't too big.

4 Fill the apples with the mixture and replace the lids. Don't worry if the lids don't fit back on . . . they're not supposed to; just sit them on top.

5 Place the apples on a steamer and set over a pot of boiling water for 8 to 10 minutes.

6 While the apples are steaming, warm the cream in a small saucepan without boiling and add the remaining Calvados.

7 To serve, cover the face of each serving plate with some of the Calvados cream. Place an apple in the centre of each plate and lean the apple lids up against the side of the fruit if you want. Drizzle the remaining Calvados cream over the apples and sprinkle with cinnamon. Serve immediately with some fine Canadian ice wine.

Recipes from Le St. Amour

For some 22 years now, chef-owner Jean-Luc Boulay has worked his culinary magic for discriminating diners at Le St. Amour on rue St.-Ursule in the heart of old Quebec City. Refreshingly, there isn't any of the snobby la-di-da-ness about him that unfortunately is all too common among "celebrity chefs" who believe their own press clippings. While Le St. Amour is one of the most celebrated restaurants in town, Chef Boulay and his front-of-house DH (designated hitter) Jacques patiently and enthusiastically assisted us while shooting into the wee hours of the morning. The atrium in the back of the restaurant is this wonderful glass-covered affair that retracts in the summer months and is full of flowers, potted trees, and plants.

Here are three wonderful recipes as featured in the closing segment of the "Quebec City Bistros" episode.

Saissie de Caribou aux Petits Fruits des Marais

	Olive oil (for frying)	
6	caribou steaks (about 1-inch/2.5-cm thick, 1/4 lb/125 g each)	6
2/3 cup	Madeira or good-quality dry red wine	150 ml
4 1/2 tbsp	good-quality brandy	65 ml
1 1/4 cups	good-quality veal stock (use beef stock in a pinch)	300 ml
1 tsp	salt	5 ml
2 tbsp	freshly cracked mixed peppercorns	30 ml
2/3 cup	wild blueberries, washed and picked over	150 ml

1 Heat olive oil in a good-sized skillet over medium-high heat until almost smoking.

2 Pan-fry the caribou steaks 2 or 3 at a time, depending on the size of your pan, until desired doneness (medium rare is the best; and if you cook them any more than medium, then substitute old tennis shoes for caribou).

3 Remove caribou from the pan, tent with tin foil, and keep warm.

4 Deglaze the pan with the Madeira and brandy, scraping up all the tasty brown bits from the pan with a wooden spoon. Reduce the liquid by half.

All good chefs, including you, take full advantage of regional and seasonal ingredients in their cooking. Chef Boulay is no exception. He gets his fabulously tender caribou meat from northern Quebec. The *"petits fruits des marais"* are small bush berries indigenous to the same region and are part of the caribou's normal diet. Chef Boulay suggests wild blueberries as a substitute. If caribou is not readily available in your neck of the woods, then try this recipe with beef tenderloin instead.

Serves 6 as a main course

5 Add stock and bring to a boil. Reduce heat and let simmer for 10 minutes. Adjust seasoning with salt and fresh cracked black pepper.
6 Return caribou to the pan and add blueberries. Heat through for 3 minutes.
7 Serve with wild rice or smashed yams and seasonal veggies.

Foie Gras à l'Armagnac

This is a very special recipe for a very special occasion. First of all, the main ingredient is foie gras, or fattened goose liver, which ain't cheap. Like sweetbreads, this is an ingredient that many people would rather just eat and not know what it is. And eat it you should, for it is an incomparable delicacy. Ask your local butcher for fresh foie gras. In Canada, it is often made with duck liver, as we have many top-drawer duck farms from one end of the country to the other (the most famous likely being Brome Lake). If you don't have any Armagnac handy, substitute the same amount of a good-quality brandy. Remember that your finished dish will only be as good as the ingredients you use.

Foie gras is also a proven aphrodisiac. Simply get naked with your lover, put on some funky tunes, consume a bottle of fine champagne (Moët & Chandon would do nicely), and feed each other this foie gras on toasted baguette. We guarantee you'll get lucky. By the by, you have to let this one sit for at least three days before serving to allow the flavours to intermingle, creating a taste overload you won't soon forget.

Serves 2 as an appetizer

Approximately 1 lb	good foie gras, preferably fresh	500 g
1/2 tsp	salt	2 ml
1/3 tsp	sugar	1.5 ml
1/4 tsp	freshly cracked black pepper	1 ml
Pinch	nutmeg	Pinch
Pinch	paprika	Pinch
1 1/2 tbsp	Armagnac or fine brandy	25 ml

1 Preheat your oven to 350°F (180°C).
2 Gently devein the foie gras without breaking it up too much.
3 In a small bowl, combine all other ingredients and add the foie gras. Cover and marinate in the fridge for at least 24 hours.
4 Put the marinated foie gras in a small earthenware or glass oven-resistant terrine and cover.
5 Put the terrine in a baking pan. Fill the pan with hot water till it reaches about two-thirds of the way up the side of the terrine.
6 Bake in the middle of the oven for about 1 hour.*
7 Cool and let sit tightly covered for at least 3 days. Serve with toasted baguette slices, champagne crackers, or Melba toast.

* Timing is a funny thing and will vary depending on your oven. When you have baked for 45 minutes, insert a candy thermometer in the middle of the foie gras. When the temperature has reached 140°F (60°C), you're done. Don't overcook or the foie gras will be grainy.

Frivolité de Saumon Fumée au Poireau et Fromage de Chèvre

2	small leeks, white and pale green	2
	parts only, with bottom cut off	
1/2 lb	goat cheese	225 g
1/4 cup	35% cream	50 ml
	Salt and freshly cracked pepper, to taste	
1 1/4 lb	smoked salmon	550 g

1 Bring a pot of salted water to boil. Boil the leeks for 3 minutes, drain, refresh under cold water, and pat very dry.

2 Run a knife vertically down the length of the leeks so that you can separate each layer as a tube (hope things aren't tube leek!). In a food processor (or using your most excellent hand mixer), mix the goat cheese well with the cream. Refrigerate for 1 hour.

3 On a sheet of plastic wrap, lay 2 sheets of the leek tube, 1 on top of the other, pressing down so that it resembles a square (if you hadn't cut the end off, it would now be the square root of leek).

4 Spread a thin layer of the cheese mixture onto the leek. Season with salt and fresh cracked pepper.

5 Lay a sheet of smoked salmon on top of the cheese mixture. Don't worry if it is not a perfect fit.

6 Using the plastic wrap as a guide, roll the whole thing up into a tight roll with the leek as the outer leaf.

7 Wrap an additional sheet of the plastic wrap around the whole thing and refrigerate for at least 1 hour and up to 6 hours so that the flavours intermingle.

8 Repeat until all the cheese filling and smoked salmon are gone.

9 Remove the plastic wrap and cut into slices using a very sharp knife. Serve on a plate with a nice vinaigrette or a splash of lemon.*

* *While not a part of Chef Boulay's original dish, this works very well when served on a crisp Indian pappadum, which you can buy at any Indian market and is a tasty addition to the ol' dinner table.*

Lac Portage and the Hunt for Moby Trout

3

We arrived at Lac Portage on the Quebec–Maine border on the eve of the last day of the fishing season. The leaves had just begun to change colour and we found ourselves in an oasis of exquisite comfort surrounded by some of the most beautiful wilderness in North America. All summer long, would-be anglers from around the world had come to this place to match wits with the crafty Canadian lake trout. Lac Portage is an exclusive fishing camp on two private lakes with all the amenities, including a classically trained chef, a top-notch wine cellar, and rustic guest cabins made of exposed timber, each one featuring a large working fireplace and oversized beds laden with huge comfy down comforters.

Now, with the first hint of winter in the air, we had but one day to capture the joys of the "trouting" experience before the season slipped away. The good folks at Lac Portage were cooperative . . . but would the trout be as accommodating?

Fly-fishing for lake trout . . . an epic battle pitting man against fish. The opposable thumb versus the swishing tail. What is it about emulating a fly dancing upon the water that stirs the romantic in people? *A River Runs Through It*. Zen and the art of fly-fishing. Perhaps it is the elegant arc of the line as it's cast with the simple snap of a wrist. Certainly the tranquility of the moment and the scenery have something to do with it. And in the end, aren't you and that elusive fish both looking for the same thing? Dinner! Besides, where else would you get to sport those cool hip waders and a fleece-lined plaid shirt?

Lac Portage Corporate Retreat is one of two operations run by Gesti-Faune Inc. (the other being Manoir Brulé) under the watchful eye of David Craig and his complement of guides and biologists. Lac Portage is everything you'd expect from a top-drawer outfitter catering to an international corporate clientele. It's a small operation with 14 sumptuously rustic cabins and an elegant main house, all looking out onto one of the two private lakes positively teeming with succulent freshwater trout.

A typical day at Lac Portage begins at dawn with a hearty breakfast and lots of strong coffee. Each angler is accompanied by his or her own personal guide. These people have tremendous respect for the wilderness in which they live and work. They see themselves as caretakers and are heavily into environmental preservation, habitat enhancement, and the development of cutting-edge fish farming. It is their solemn responsibility to put back what they take out. This is an example of preserving a wonderful natural resource at its best.

Meanwhile, back at the main lodge, award-winning chef Jean-François Lacroix and his team are readying themselves for your return, whereupon they will clean and prepare your day's catch for dinner, as accompanied by a fine selection of wines, ports, and digestifs. Stuffed and sated, you may then retire to the drawing room or the front porch and contemplate the day's adventures. Somewhere on the lake a loon calls out. You trundle back to your cabin for a well-earned sleep under a handmade duvet to dream about the one that got away and that which awaits you on the morrow.

In the end, Carlo did not catch ol' Moby Trout. Legend has it he's still out there playfully toying with anglers, growing plumper, juicier . . . and smarter.

Here are the recipes from, and inspired by, Executive Chef Jean-François's kitchen as featured in the "Moby Trout" episode. Trout is one fish that is available fresh from one end of the country to the other. Enjoy.

Pumpkin Soup

6	slices bacon	6	**Serves 6**
2 tbsp	unsalted butter	30 ml	
1	small onion, diced	1	
1	stalk of celery, diced	1	
2 tsp	flour	10 ml	
1 cup	chicken stock	250 ml	
1 cup	2% milk	250 ml	
Pinch	nutmeg	Pinch	
Pinch	paprika	Pinch	
1 quart	canned pumpkin purée	1 L	
1 cup	35% cream	250 ml	

1 Cook bacon until crispy. Remove bacon from skillet and set aside.
2 In a soup pot, melt butter over a medium heat. Add onion and celery and sauté until translucent, about 6 minutes.
3 Add flour and mix well, creating a roux. Cook for 1 minute until golden brown.
4 Increase heat and add chicken stock and milk. Bring to a boil and lower heat. Add nutmeg and paprika. Simmer uncovered for 20 minutes.
5 Add pumpkin purée and cook for another 5 minutes.
6 Purée soup in a blender (be careful with hot liquids) and strain into another soup pot through a fine sieve, pushing down on solids with the back of a wooden spoon.
7 Reheat soup without bringing to a boil. Add cream and warm.
8 Ladle soup into bowls and sprinkle with crumbled bacon.

Truite en Colère avec Sauce Beurre Blanc

Get to know your fishmonger. When he cleans the fish for you, make sure he gives you the bones, as you'll need them to make the stock. Don't skimp on the quality of wine you cook with. Remember that your finished dish will only be as good as the ingredients you put into it.

Serves 6 as a main course

2/3 lb	northern pike or other white fish fillets, skinned, bones reserved	300 g
2	egg whites	2
1 1/2 cups	35% cream	375 ml
	Salt, white pepper, and freshly cracked black pepper, to taste	
1/2 lb	carrots, diced	225 g
1/2 lb	onion, diced	225 g
1/2 lb	celery stalk, diced	225 g
1/2 lb	leek, white part only, diced	225 g
Approximately 1 lb	cold unsalted butter	450 g
1 1/4 cups	good dry white wine	300 ml
3 quarts	cold water	3 L
1	sprig fresh rosemary (or 1 tsp/5 ml dried)	1
1	sprig fresh thyme (or 1 tsp/5 ml dried)	1
1	sprig fresh savory (or 1 tsp/5 ml dried)	1
2	bunches fresh spinach	2
6	12-inch/30-cm rainbow trout, cleaned and deboned, heads and tails left on	6

For the stuffing:

1 Reduce the white fish fillet to a fine purée in a food processor.
2 Add egg whites and mix well.
3 Add 1 ¼ cups (300 ml) of the cream in a light drip through the food processor spout as you would add oil to mayonnaise. Do not overbeat.
4 Add salt and white pepper to taste.
5 Meanwhile, blanch the diced carrots in a saucepan for 4 minutes, refresh under cold water, and pat dry.
6 Using a spatula, scrape the purée into a bowl and mix in carrots. Refrigerate.

For the fish stock:

1 In a large saucepan, sauté onion, celery, and leek in 2 tbsp (30 ml) of unsalted butter for 4 minutes over medium heat.
2 Add the fish bones and cook for 4 minutes longer.
3 Add the white wine, water, and herbs. Bring to a boil and simmer for 30 minutes. Put through a fine strainer into another saucepan, pushing on the solids with a spoon to get all of the stock.

For the spinach:

1 Clean spinach and remove stems, keeping the leaves whole.
2 Heat a kettle full of water.
3 Put the spinach in a large pot and pour in the boiling water. Cover and let sit for 5 minutes.
4 Drain the water and refresh the spinach in cold water for 3 minutes. Drain again and dry spinach.

For the trout:

1 Preheat your oven to 350°F (180°C).
2 Place the trout on their backs, the bellies open and flat towards you, the heads pointing away. Pat dry and season with salt and fresh cracked pepper.
3 Cover the fish in a layer of spinach.
4 Place a large spoonful of the white fish stuffing in the middle of the spinach bed.
5 Bring the tail of each trout towards the head, as if folding the fish in half.
6 Insert the tail into the head cavity and pull it through the fish's mouth until it makes a tight bundle. Flip the fish over so their heads are up.
7 Bring stock to a boil in an ovenproof pan large enough to hold all the trout with at least ½ inch (1 cm) between them.

8 Once the stock is boiling, remove from heat, add the trout, and place in the oven for 15 minutes.

9 Remove pan from oven. Turn the heat off. Place trout on an oven-proof platter and tent with tin foil. Place in oven to keep warm.

For the sauce:

1 Strain remaining stock into a small saucepan.

2 Add remaining cream. Bring to a boil and simmer for about 15 minutes or until reduced by half.

3 Turn heat to low and add remaining butter in small pieces, one at a time and whisking well. Wait until one piece of butter has melted before adding the next.

4 Don't let the sauce boil. Add salt and white pepper to taste.

To serve:

1 Pour the sauce on the plate first, then add the trout.

2 Serve with roasted new potatoes, basmati rice, or couscous.

The Nutty Trout

If *Truite en Colère* seems a bit too elaborate, here is a wonderful super-fast trout recipe instead. As always, make sure you start with the freshest Canadian trout possible.

Serves 6 as a main course

1/4 cup	pine nuts	50 ml
1/4 cup	pecans	50 ml
1 tbsp	bread crumbs	15 ml
1 tbsp	finely diced fresh parsley	15 ml
6	trout fillets, skin on	6
	Salt and freshly cracked pepper	
3 tbsp	unsalted butter	45 ml
1	garlic clove, finely diced	1
4–6 tbsp	vegetable oil (for frying)	60–90 ml

1 Chop the pine nuts and pecans. You can do this in a food processor or using the appropriate attachment on your handy-dandy hand mixer. You can also put the nuts in a resealable plastic bag, cover it with a dishtowel, turn your thoughts to tax time, and wail away on the nuts with a hammer or tenderizing mallet. Pour the chopped nuts into a bowl and mix in the bread crumbs and parsley. Whichever method of pulverizing you use, don't go overboard or you'll end up with a paste consistency.

2 Pat the trout fillets dry with paper towel and season with salt and fresh cracked pepper. Arrange the fillets on a baking sheet, skin-side-down and in a single layer.

3 Melt the butter in a small saucepan over medium heat and add the garlic. Sauté for 2 to 3 minutes or until the garlic is nicely browned and the pungent aroma attracts a crowd.

4 Brush the trout fillets with the garlic butter and sprinkle with the nut mixture. Make sure you cover the entire face of the fillets.

5 Tightly wrap the baking pan in plastic wrap so that it is pushing down on the fillets. Refrigerate for at least 1 hour.

6 Preheat your oven to 400°F (200°C).

7 Melt half of the vegetable oil in a large skillet over a medium-high heat until almost smoking. Add 3 of the trout fillets, nutty-crust-side-down and pan-fry for 2 minutes without moving. Watch out: *It is vedy vedy importanto* that the trout are not crowded into the skillet, as this will affect cooking time. Make sure the fillets are separated by at least ¾ inch (2 cm), or just pan-fry 2 at a time instead.

8 When the first batch is done, transfer them back to the baking sheet. Place them on the sheet skin-side-down to reveal a wonderful golden-brown nutty crust with flecks of parsley green. Yummy! Be careful not to flip them over too roughly as the nut crust might break away. Repeat the process until all the fillets are pan-fried.

9 Place the baking sheet in the middle of the oven and bake for a mere 5 minutes. The fillets aren't that thick and there's nothing worse than overcooked dry trout . . . okay, overcooked dry chicken might be worse, but you get the idea.

10 Place each trout fillet nut-side-up on a serving plate. In the summer we suggest serving this on a very large bed of mixed greens with a vinaigrette made from flavoured vinegar (such as strawberry or shallot-infused vinegar available for a couple of bucks at most large grocery stores) and a nut oil (such as walnut or sesame).

In winter consider raisin and parsley studded basmati rice. In either case, the rice or greens should act as a pedestal upon which you place your creation!

Grilled Sea Bass with Watermelon-Mango Salsa

You can easily substitute a nice swordfish steak or a red snapper fillet for the sea bass if you'd like. A great piece of fresh fish needs minimum cooking, so we recommend grilling or broiling whenever possible. The secret to the salsa is in the size of the chunks. You don't want the watermelon chunks to be too small or they'll get mooshy. On the other hand, you do want your cucumber to be no more than a quarter of the size of the watermelon chunks to achieve the proper balance of crunchiness (generally known in scientific circles as the CQ, or crunchy coefficient). And so we can conclude that, as with all things related to the cucumber, size does matter. But seriously, this salsa is wonderful to look at – full of watermelon pink, burnt orange from the mango, bright red from the chili, purple from the onion, green from the cilantro, and white from the cucumber. It looks incredible when set upon a canvas of white fish.

Serves 6 as a main course

How to Cut a Mango:

1 Cut a bit of the top and bottom off the mango so that it can stand flat on your work surface.
2 Working from top to bottom, run a good paring knife down the side of the mango, peeling away the skin as you would with a potato.
3 Again working from top to bottom, cut the mango away from the pit in long slices... voilà.

3	slices seedless watermelon, cut into 1-inch/2.5-cm cubes	3
2	mangoes, coarsely chopped	2
1/2	medium red onion, thinly sliced	1/2
1/2	English cucumber, peeled, halved, seeded, and cut into 1/4-inch/0.5-cm cubes	1/2
1	fresh hot pepper (such as Thai or jalapeño), seeded and diced	1
	Juice of 3 limes	
6 tbsp	olive oil	90 ml
6 tbsp	fresh cilantro, stems removed and coarsely chopped	90 ml
6	sea bass fillets, skin on	6
	Salt and freshly cracked pepper	
18	chive stalks (for garnish)	18

1 Combine the watermelon, mango, onion, cucumber, hot pepper, lime juice, 4 tbsp (60 ml) olive oil, and cilantro in a bowl and set aside for 30 minutes so that the tastes combine.
2 Brush the skin side of the sea bass with remaining olive oil and season with salt and freshly cracked pepper. Grill or broil the fish to your liking, 4 to 6 minutes per side, depending on thickness.
3 To serve, plate the fish fillets and top with a heaping spoonful of the salsa, letting it fall from the fish onto the plate. Insert 3 chive stalks into the centre of each salsa mound so that they stand upright and fan out a bit. This dish looks so great that we wouldn't put anything else on the plate. Take care of your starch portion of the meal with a soup or separate appetizer. If you really have to go with a starch in the main course, we suggest a bed of basmati rice mixed with chopped roasted almonds, dried cranberries, and diced fresh cilantro, upon which you plate the fish and then the salsa.

Seasons in Thyme

We've stuffed ourselves on lots of fab food while shooting *The Great Canadian Food Show*. From coast to coast to coast we have been shown tremendous warmth and hospitality by the people who allowed us into their lives for a brief albeit hectic time.

Of all the places we visited and all the food we ate in the six months we travelled across Canada, the single most memorable taste experience I had was sitting in Paul Offer's organic veggie garden in Thyne Valley, Prince Edward Island. It was a beautiful warm July day and Paul's place was one of the stops we made as we followed hot young chef Stefan Czapalay around as he picked up fresh local produce for that evening's island-tasting menu.

Stef and his beautiful, smart-as-a-whip wife Sharlene had opened a 60-seat restaurant in the small village (population 400) in Thyne Valley outside of Summerside. Well off the main highway and in the opposite direction from all the green-gabled touristo stuff, Seasons in Thyme was a culinary oasis in a desert of deep-fried glop.

P.E.I. gives up some of the most incredible produce in Canada; it's too bad that little of it actually stays on the island. It is sadly ironic that almost all of the fantastic food P.E.I. produces is shipped elsewhere in order for its residents to make a living. The best oysters in the world come from Malpeque Bay, and the best Malpeque oysters come from the Burleigh Brothers, a mere golf swing away from Thyne Valley. Stef and Sharlene are two of only a few locals who buy the Burleighs' succulent bivalves. Everything else goes to the United States, Montreal, or Torontosaurus Rex. These are the most amazing oysters on the face of the earth. Yes, British Columbia has a wider variety of oysters with a greater range of tastes, but the Malpeque is undoubtedly the mother of all oysters. A Malpeque oyster is big, thick, and meaty with an indescribably slippery aftertaste that puts your taste buds into orbit. So there we were in Paul Offer's three-acre organic farmers garden, shooting Stef as he chose the greens and veggies for the big dinner that night. Once you get past his gruff, no-compromise exterior, Paul is a really nice guy. Here's someone who knows what he likes and knows what he wants, the rest of the world be damned. On his small island farm you will find dozens of varieties of lettuce, beets, squash, tomatoes, beans, and carrots. I remember him saying that he can grow a big juicy hybrid tomato with a delicate ruby red flesh that requires the same handling as a newborn because his produce goes down the road instead of into a big cardboard box to be shipped halfway around the world. No iceberg lettuce here.

By the time this book is published Stef and Sharlene will have packed up and moved into Summerside, where they have built themselves a spanking new restaurant (still called Seasons in Thyme). If you go in the summer, do yourself a favour and call ahead for reservations.

Chicken Ballentine with Carrot Butter and Beet Emulsions

"Ballentine" refers to the great postmodernist impresario George Ballentine, who once walked into the 22 Club and said, "Hey, somebody roll me up a stuffed chicken breast so dat it looks like a cigar and be quick about it!" Okay, so we have no idea what "Ballentine" refers to, but it coulda happened our way. This is Stefan's signature recipe, which he created for the 1998 Culinary World Cup in Melbourne, Australia. Fresh beet and carrot juices are readily available at health food stores. If you don't have Melfour vinegar, substitute the same quantity of tarragon vinegar or sherry vinegar. By the way, the little juicy bit that detaches from the underside of a chicken breast is called the tenderloin.

Serves 6 as a main course

6	chicken breasts, skin removed	6
	Salt and freshly cracked pepper, to taste	
1/3 cup	good dry sherry	75 ml
Approximately 1 cup	35% cream	250 ml
1/2 lb	unsalted butter	225 g
6	chicken legs, deboned, diced, and skin removed	6
3	large shallots, minced	3
24	mushrooms, sliced	24
30	green peppercorns	30
5 tbsp	good dry white wine	75 ml
1 1/4 cups	carrot juice	300 ml
1/3 cup	Melfour vinegar	75 ml
1 1/4 cups	beet juice	300 ml
1/3 cup	red wine vinegar	75 ml

1 Preheat your oven to 375°F (190°C).
2 Remove the tenderloin (the juicy bit clinging to the underside of the deboned breast) from each of the chicken breasts.

3 Butterfly and cut the chicken breasts until they are rectangular, twice as long as they are wide, about 6 x 3 inches (15 x 7 cm). To butterfly, you simply cut a couple of slits lengthwise in the bottom side of each breast and cover it in plastic wrap. Then you take a tenderizing mallet, a bottle, or the back side of a good heavy knife and pound on the chicken while thinking of your ex, the taxman, or Yoko Ono.

4 Pat the breasts dry and season with salt and fresh cracked pepper.

5 Purée the tenderloins, chicken scraps, sherry, and 1/3 cup (75 ml) of the cream until smooth. Season with salt and fresh cracked pepper.

6 In a large skillet, melt 5 tbsp (75 ml) of the unsalted butter over a medium-high heat. Add the diced chicken legs and shallots. Reduce heat to medium and gently sauté for about 10 minutes.

7 Add mushrooms and peppercorns. Mix well and cook for another 5 minutes.

8 Remove from the stove-top and pour into a large bowl. Cool thoroughly and add the chicken mousse from the food processor.

9 Fill the chicken breasts along the lengths of the pieces with some of the mousse mixture and roll gently into a cigar shape. Sprinkle with white wine.

10 Wrap each rolled breast in parchment paper and then tin foil.

11 Bake in the oven for about 12 minutes. Remove from the oven and let sit for 10 minutes so that the juices settle in the meat.

12 After you put the chicken in the oven, bring the carrot juice and Melfour vinegar to boil in one saucepan, and bring the beet juice and red wine vinegar to boil in another. Reduce both liquids for 10 to 15 minutes or until they've reduced to 1/4 of their original volume.

13 Add half of the remaining cream to each pan and boil for 2 minutes longer. Add remaining butter and whisk thoroughly.

14 Remove chicken from foil and parchment paper and plate. Drizzle both sauces around the chicken. The offsetting colours of the two emulsions will look great on the plate. Serve the chicken on a bed of basmati rice with baby green peas and finely diced sweet red pepper.

6 Things You Can Do with a Head of Iceberg Lettuce

- Set iceberg lettuce on fire and hurl from the turret of your castle at attacking Visigoths .
- Pack fine antique china in shredded iceberg lettuce for cross-country shipping.
- Wrap iceberg lettuce in duct tape for instant tetherball.
- Shred iceberg lettuce and enter it in a tastes-like-wet-newspaper contest.
- Leave shredded iceberg lettuce lying around your backyard, thus forcing pesky raccoons and squirrels to seek edible food elsewhere.
- Send iceberg lettuce to developing countries as an example of what happens when technology goes oh so wrong.

Asparagus Soup with Chive Oil

For some reason the French think it's chi-chi to bury this wonderful perennial so as to produce an albino version. Whether it makes your pee stink or not (apparently a curiosity of science visited on about half of us), asparagus soup is awesome hot or cold. The secret to the intense flavour in this recipe is the use of the otherwise crappy asparagus ends in the stock.

Serves 6

2 lbs	fresh asparagus	1 kg
4 cups	water	1 L
3 tbsp	olive oil	45 ml
1	small onion, chopped	1
1	garlic bud, diced	1
4 cups	chicken stock	1 L
1 cup	canola oil	250 ml
1	bunch fresh chives	1
	Salt, white pepper, and freshly cracked pepper	

1 Separate the crappy grey-white part of each asparagus spear from the lovely green end. You can do this by holding one end of the spear in each hand and gently bending until it snaps at its natural point of resistance. Repeat with the rest of the asparagus.

2 Bring the water to a gentle boil and toss in the crappy grey-white bits. Reduce the heat and cover. Simmer for at least 30 minutes or until the asparagus is really mooshy. Discard the grey-white bits and save the asparagus stock (as opposed to the asparagus stalks, which you've also saved).

3 In a soup pot, heat the olive oil over a medium-high heat and add the onion. Sauté for 3 minutes and add the garlic. Sauté for 1 minute longer and add the asparagus. Cook 5 or 6 minutes longer as the asparagus begins to sweat and develops an intense, amazing shade of green you wish you could use to repaint the bathroom.

4 Add both stocks, partially cover, and cook over medium-low heat for 30 minutes, stirring occasionally.

5 While the soup is bubbling, purée the canola oil and chives. Add salt and fresh cracked pepper to taste and refrigerate.

6 When the 30 minutes are up, purée the soup and season to taste with salt and white pepper (black pepper will mess with the perfect green colour you have now achieved).

7 To serve, ladle the soup into bowls and drizzle with the chive oil.

Another option is to reduce the soup by gently boiling for 45 minutes and then adding cream. Refrigerate and serve cold. Cold cooked shrimp also work well with this soup.

Stefan's Mushroom Flan

6	large eggs	6
Approximately 1/2 lb	assorted mushrooms	225 g
	(such as shiitake,	
	portobello, crimini, cepe)	
3 tbsp	clarified butter	45 ml
1 cup	35% cream	250 ml
	Salt and pepper, to taste	
6	large white mushroom caps (as egg holders)	6
2 tbsp	finely ground dried porcini mushrooms	30 ml
2 tbsp	finely diced parsley	30 ml

1 Preheat your oven to 350°F (180°C).
2 Carefully crack the eggs about a quarter of the way down the shell. Pour egg out of shell into a bowl. Carefully rinse out the inside of the shells and return them to the carton with lid cut off.
3 Finely dice the mushrooms and sauté in clarified butter for 6 minutes over medium heat until the mushrooms are soft and their flavour has infused the butter.
4 Increase heat and add cream. Bring to a bubble and reduce heat. Simmer for 5 minutes.
5 Strain through a fine sieve into a small saucepan. Let flan mixture cool.
6 Pour flan mixture into eggs and mix well with whisk. Add salt and fresh cracked pepper to taste.
7 Carefully pour the egg and flan mixture back into the shells sitting in the egg carton.
8 Sit egg carton in a roasting pan and fill the pan with boiling water until two-thirds of the way up the side of the carton.
9 Place pan in the oven and cook for 10 to 12 minutes, depending on your oven, until the custards have set. Don't overcook!
10 Using a grapefruit spoon or paring knife, take the 6 large white mushroom caps and shave off a bit of the rounded side of the cap, so that it can sit upside down on a plate as a fungi-holder for your egg.
11 Place a mushroom cap on a serving plate and, carefully using tongs, transfer an egg so that it sits in the middle of the mushroom cap. Garnish the plate with a sprinkle of the dried mushroom dust and diced parsley. Serve immediately.

This was the first thing I ever tasted from Stefan's kitchen and I immediately knew I was on to someone special. This is actually way easier to make than it looks and has a wonderful woodsy taste that'll blow you away.

To clarify the butter, melt it in a small saucepan and then skim off the foam on the top. What's left is the golden clear-drawn butter, which you then separate from the milk solids that have settled at the bottom of the pan. In Indian cooking, clarified butter is called *ghee*. Trust me, it's worth the effort, as it gives the butter a wonderful nutty flavour and a much higher smoking point.

Serves 6 as an appetizer

Adventures in Chinatown 5

Not so long ago, your average Canadian thought Chinese food meant chicken balls or chop suey. A regular MSG-fest, free delivery, or six free egg rolls with every order over twenty bucks. Nowadays, thanks in part to an enlightened immigration policy over lo these past few decades, things have changed considerably for the better. Asian is "in" and chi-chi-la-la restaurants are doing "fusion" cuisine, where East meets West with some decidedly fantastic results. There is a very good chance that your home town has a number of different pan-Pacific restaurants and grocery stores to choose from. Ginger root, fresh coriander, red chili paste, and bok choy are fairly regular staples in many a Canadian pantry these days. Thank god.

Toronto and Vancouver have been feuding for some time now as to which city has the second-largest "Chinatown" in North America (the biggest by far is in San Francisco), while most larger Canadian cities and towns now have an area of visible Asian influence similarly misnamed. The term "Chinatown" goes back to the good old days when Chinese labourers were brought over to North America to work in abject poverty while building the railway lines. While Canada did not condone slavery per se, the way Asian immigrants were treated was almost as bad. In fact, they were not all Chinese, we just called them that because they all looked alike to your average railway baron.

Mercifully, we have come a long way in the last hundred years. Hot and sour soup, kimchee, and pad Thai are as welcome at the table as tourtière and baked beans. But the term "Chinatown" remains and is now used as benignly as "Little Italy" or "The Latin Quarter."

We decided to shoot our story about the wonderful diversity of pan-Asian influences on Canadian cuisine in Vancouver. We had an interesting juxtaposition to deal with in framing the story for this episode. Whether

Thai, Vietnamese, Chinese, or whatever, we were dealing with some of the oldest and most vibrant cultures in the world, complete with diverse culinary histories and traditions. Even to say "Asian cuisine" is akin to suggesting that there is such a thing as "European cuisine" (or even a singular "Canadian cuisine" for that matter!). Thai and Cantonese cuisines are as diverse as German and Italian. In Canada, we measure our history in decades (with apologies to the First Nations), while these pan-Asian cultures work on the order of millennia. Yet here, in North America, mainstream pan-Asian influences are a relatively new thing, since the majority of immigrants from that part of the world arrived only in the last 50 years. The oldest cultures give forth the newest immigrants. What goes around comes around.

So, it is no small wonder that a stroll through a neighbourhood Asian market can be at once an adventure and intimidating to your average third-generation non-Asian Canadian. Of course, those recently arrived from Singapore might be confused upon their first visit to a Jewish deli or an Italian botega. Consider someone from Itoman, Japan, being presented with charred and diced pig entrails smothered in a tomato-vinegar concoction for the first time (translation: Bar-b-qued Bratwurst on a bun with ketchup).

Once again we encourage you, if you have not already, to embrace the culinary treasures the world has laid at your feet. Wander around an Asian market and immerse yourself in the staccato metre of absolutely foreign dialects. Stroll the aisles and consider bags of dried fish, pickled this, and spiced that. Fondle and smell large arthritic-looking veggies and fruit of the prickly and persnickety variety. Happen upon the fish and meat counter, and before you withdraw at the sight of a heaping basket of chicken feet or bug-eyed fish, remember that the Italians do interesting things with pigs' cheeks, the French with livers and gizzards, and the Irish with many a sheep's unmentionables. Not to mention the made-in-Canada delicacies of cod tongues, beaver tails, seal flippers, and prairie oysters! In the culinary universe, gentle reader, one truly can make a silken-tasting purse from a sow's ear, preferably served up in a nice roasted red pepper purée. On the other hand, if you happen to be of pan-Asian descent or an aficionado of that cuisine, and you see some brave lost soul wandering the aisles of your local Asian market, give them a hail-and-well-met and show them where the kimchee is.

Thai Spicy Coconut Soup (*Tom Kha Gai*)

This is one of our favourite soups in the world. It is at once complex and unique in its layered tastes. You've got your hot and spicy, your sweet and sour, and your creamy coconut all in one bowl. This classic soup is to Thai cuisine what pasta is to Italian . . . which is to say that there are numerous regional variations. This recipe is a compilation of a number of different Tom Kha Gai's we've tried. The heat quotient in this version is kept low so that everyone can enjoy the soup, so adjust the number of Thai chilies to suit your personal tastes.

Serves 6 as a starter

Thai Ingredients

If you can't find Thai chilies, substitute any good hot pepper or some garlic chili paste. Galangal looks very much like ginger but has a spicier taste (it's also known as Thai ginger) and can be found fresh in your local Asian market. No galangal? Substitute a bit more ginger. Fresh Kaffir lime leaves are a bit difficult to find on a regular basis in most Canadian cities (although when you walk into an Asian market and are carried away by the citrus aroma that perfumes the air and makes everyone happy, chances are there are some fresh Kaffir limes in stock, so check it out) but the dried variety only cost a couple of bucks and will last for a year in your pantry. If you can't find Kaffir lime leaves, substitute the rind of one lime, coarsely chopped.

No cheesecloth?

An easy and inexpensive substitute for cheesecloth is a sheet of J-cloth. Just make sure it's a new one!

12	very large shrimp, peeled and deveined, shells reserved	12
1	1-inch/2.5-cm piece of galangal, skin on, sliced into medallions	1
1	1-inch/2.5-cm piece of ginger, skin on, sliced into medallions	1
5	Kaffir lime leaves	5
2	stalks lemon grass, tender bottom (approximately 6 inches/15 cm), coarsely chopped	2
1 1/4 cups	canned coconut milk	300 ml
2 1/2 cups	chicken stock	625 ml
6	large shiitake mushroom caps, cleaned and stems removed	6
1	Thai chili, coarsely chopped	1
4 tbsp	lime juice	60 ml
4 tbsp	Asian fish sauce	60 ml
4 tsp	sugar	20 ml
1/2	red bell pepper, cut into long thin slices	1/2
	Fresh coriander, stems removed and coarsely chopped (for garnish)	

1 Fold a large piece of cheesecloth onto your work surface. In the middle of the cloth, place the shrimp shells, galangal, ginger, Kaffir lime leaves, and lemon grass. Tie the cloth securely with some cooking string. You have just created an Asian bouquet garni (which is French for overpriced herbs tied up in cheesecloth).

2 Combine the coconut milk and chicken stock in a soup pot. Sometimes the solids in the coconut milk will separate from the liquid while sitting on the shelf. Not to worry. Simply scoop out all the solids and add them to the pot. Turn the heat on at medium-high and whisk the liquids so that they are well blended. Bring to a gentle boil and reduce the heat to medium so that it's juuuuust bubbling nicely. Drop in your bag of goodies and cover. Let simmer for 40 minutes.

3 Add the shrimp, mushrooms, chili, lime juice, fish sauce, and sugar and simmer for 10 minutes longer or until the shrimp are just done. Remove and throw out the cheesecloth bag.

4 To serve, place 2 shrimp and 1 mushroom cap in each of 6 serving bowls, along with a few slices of red bell pepper. Ladle the broth over top and sprinkle with fresh coriander. Serve immediately.

Vietnamese Beef and Shrimp Noodle Soup

1/3 lb	bean thread noodles or vermicelli	150 g
1 1/4 quarts	beef stock (low-sodium, preferably)	1.25 L
1 1/4 quarts	chicken stock (low-sodium, if possible)	1.25 L
1	large onion, halved and thinly sliced	1
2 tbsp	fish sauce	30 ml
6	jumbo shrimp (or 12 large shrimp), precooked and peeled, shells reserved	6
4	garlic cloves, coarsely chopped	4
1	2-inch/5-cm piece of ginger, skin on and coarsely chopped	1
3	star anise	3
1	red pepper, halved and thinly sliced	1
1 cup	coarsely chopped assorted mushrooms, stems removed	250 ml
3/4 lb	flank steak, sliced very thin against the grain and seasoned with freshly cracked pepper	350 g
	Juice of 1/2 lemon	
1/2	bunch fresh cilantro, stems removed and roughly chopped	1/2

1 Bring a large pot of water to boil over a high heat and add the noodles. Cook the noodles for about 1 or 2 minutes or until al dente.

2 Drain the noodles immediately and rinse them under cold water. Drain again once they've cooled off. Set aside.

3 Combine the beef stock, chicken stock, onion, fish sauce, shrimp shells, garlic, ginger, and star anise in a large soup pot and bring to a boil over medium-high heat. Bring the heat down to medium and simmer for 25 minutes. Strain the broth through a fine sieve. Do it twice if you have to because you want to end up with a nice clear broth with nothing floating in it.

4 Return the broth to the soup pot and bring to a rapid boil. Once it starts boiling, turn the heat off and add the red pepper, mushrooms, beef slices, shrimp, and lemon juice. Cover immediately and let sit for 5 minutes.

5 While the soup is steeping and the beef is cooking, divide the noodles into 6 large soup bowls. Ladle the soup over the noodles, making sure everybody gets some beef and shrimp. Garnish with fresh cilantro and pass around some good-quality hot sauce for those who want to go spicyamoondo. Serve with frosty cold beer.

Not surprisingly, there are a lot of variations on the theme of Vietnamese beef noodle soup. In this one, we've added shrimp for variety, red pepper and cilantro for colour, and mushrooms for texture. You'll need very big soup bowls, or put the pot in the middle of the table so that everyone can have seconds. The only special ingredients you need are the fish sauce (see the Cold Shrimp and Noodle Salad recipe in this chapter for details), bean thread noodles, and star anise. You can replace the bean thread noodles (which are thin, tender, transparent, and probably just down the aisle from the fish sauce) with vermicelli, which has to cook a minute or so longer. Star anise is a wonderful star-shaped pod with a spicy licorice kick to it. You can buy it dried for very little money in your local Asian market. The soup will work without it, but it's worth having in your pantry. It lasts practically forever when kept in an airtight bag and also can be used to flavour tea and as a breath mint.

Serves 6 as a main course

Dim Sum Shrimp Dumplings with Three Dipping Sauces

These Chinese dumplings are an Asian variation of the perogies made famous by the ladies of Kamsack, Saskatchewan (see Chapter 7), or is it the other way around? Then there are Italian gnocchi and several other stuffed packets of tasty treats from the four corners of the globe. Most of these cuisines developed independent of each other, and all came up with the same good-to-eat idea. Once more we see that what's old is new, what's exotic is familiar. Chinese five spice powder is available at all Asian markets and most health or bulk food stores. A bottle of sake (rice wine) is readily available in your local liquor store for roughly the same price as a bottle of table wine. As the recipe that follows calls for a small amount, heat the remaining bottle of sake in a pot of boiling water and serve warm with this dish instead of wine. Keep the stack of won ton wrappers under a damp tea towel while you're stuffing them so that they don't dry out.

Serves 6 as an appetizer

1	head broccoli, florets only, diced	1
1	carrot, peeled and diced	1
1/2 lb	medium shrimp, peeled, deveined, and coarsely chopped	225 g
2	garlic cloves, diced	2
3	shallots, diced	3
1/4 tsp	Chinese five spice powder	1 ml
2 tbsp	soy sauce	30 ml
1 tsp	fish sauce	5 ml
2 tbsp	sake	30 ml
2 tbsp	diced fresh coriander, stems removed	30 ml
2 tbsp	diced fresh basil, stems removed	30 ml
30	round won ton wrappers	30
2	egg whites, whisked	2
6	baby bib lettuce or romaine	6
	Lettuce leaves (for garnish)	
	Chopped chives (for garnish)	

1 Blanch the broccoli and carrots in a pot of salted boiling water for 30 seconds, then cool them off in a bowl of ice water to stop the cooking process.

2 Combine the veggies, shrimp, garlic, shallots, five spice powder, soy sauce, fish sauce, sake, coriander, and basil in a food processor. Blend the ingredients, pulsing the processor on and off, until you have a fine mixture.

3 Bring a pot of water to boil over high heat. Place a won ton wrapper on the work surface before you and brush its edges with the egg wash. Mound a heaping teaspoonful of the shrimp and veggie mixture onto the middle of the wrapper and fold it over on itself so that you've made yourself a half moon. Pick the won ton up and pinch the edges closed, forcing any air out of the packet. Repeat until dumplings are prepared.

4 Boil the dumplings in 3 batches for about 2 minutes each or until they rise to the top (just like the perogies!). Transfer the dumplings to a covered bowl and keep warm while you boil the other batches.

5 To serve, place a lettuce leaf on each of the serving plates. Put

5 dumplings on each of the lettuce leaves and sprinkle with some chives. Serve immediately with the three dipping sauces in the middle of the table or in small individual serving bowls that you can pick up for no money at any Asian grocery store. While you're at it, take away the forks and serve the dumplings with chopsticks, also cheap, cheap, cheap at the same Asian store.

Sesame Ginger Dipping Sauce

1/2 cup	sake	125 ml
2 tbsp	sesame oil	30 ml
1	garlic clove, finely minced	1
1 tbsp	finely diced fresh ginger	15 ml
1 tbsp	finely diced fresh chives	15 ml

Combine all the ingredients at least 30 minutes before serving.

Peanut Dipping Sauce

Red curry sauce is available at most Asian markets and is an excellent addition to your pantry. If none is available, use the same quantity of your favourite hot sauce, although the resulting peanut sauce will not have the same depth of flavour.

4 tbsp	roasted unsalted peanuts	60 ml
2 cups	canned coconut milk	500 ml
1 tbsp	red curry sauce	15 ml
1 tsp	sugar	5 ml
	Juice of 1/2 lemon	
1 tbsp	fish sauce	15 ml

1 Grind the peanuts to a fine meal in a food processor.
2 Bring the coconut milk to a boil in a small saucepan over high heat and add the curry sauce and peanuts. Reduce heat to medium and simmer for 15 minutes, or until reduced by half.
3 Add the sugar, lemon juice, and fish sauce and reduce heat to low. Cover and cook for 10 minutes without letting the sauce boil. Purée with a hand mixer or in a blender. Adjust to taste with more lemon juice, sugar, or fish sauce. If the sauce is too thick, add a bit of water or additional coconut milk. Serve this sauce hot.

Sweet and Sour Sauce

Garlic chili sauce is available at all Asian grocery stores and many supermarkets. Once you've got it in your fridge, you'll find yourself using it to flavour many dishes and as a spicy condiment for sandwiches.

1 cup	rice vinegar	250 ml
1 cup	sugar	250 ml
3 tbsp	soy sauce	45 ml
1 tsp	fish sauce	5 ml
1–2 tbsp	garlic chili sauce (or more, depending on how hot you want it)	15–30 ml
2	garlic cloves, finely diced	2

1 Heat the vinegar in a small saucepan over medium-high heat, but do not let it come to a boil. The vapour from the heated vinegar will clear out your sinuses and take the enamel off your teeth.
2 Add the sugar and stir until it dissolves. Add the soy sauce and fish sauce and lower the heat to medium. Let the sauce cook at a gentle boil for 15 minutes, or until it begins to thicken.
3 Add the garlic chili sauce and garlic and stir to mix well. Remove from heat and cool to room temperature before serving.

Marinated Asian Flank Steak

Flank steak is a very inexpensive cut of meat. The secret here is in the marinating, which breaks down the fibrous content of the steak, making it melt-in-your-mouth tender. The longer you marinate the meat, the better the taste will be. This is a great weeknight dinner because it takes no time to prepare . . . a little marinating . . . a little cooking . . . badabee badaboom, you're done! Do not use a metal bowl for the marinating, as the marinade will react to the metal and ruin the meat. This one also works major domo on the bar-b-que.

Serves 6 as a main course

1/2 cup	soy sauce	125 ml
1/3 cup	Worcestershire sauce	75 ml
3 tbsp	oyster sauce	45 ml
	Juice of 1 lemon	
2 tbsp	finely minced fresh ginger	30 ml
2 lbs	flank steak	1 kg

1 Combine the soy sauce, Worcestershire sauce, oyster sauce, lemon juice, and ginger in a glass baking dish large enough to hold the steak.
2 Add the steak and bathe all sides in the marinade. Let stand for 1 hour at room temperature or overnight in the fridge. If you marinate overnight, make sure you return the meat to room temperature before cooking, as this will affect cooking time.
3 Preheat your broiler until it's good and hot.
4 Broil the steak for 7 minutes per side for medium rare.
5 While the steak is broiling, pour the leftover marinade into a skillet, bring to a boil over a medium-high heat, then simmer on a low heat for 5 minutes.
6 Transfer the steak to a cutting board and let stand for 10 minutes so that the internal juices will settle. Slice lengthwise across the grain.

7 Just before serving, place the steak, one serving at a time, into the reduced marinade for a few seconds just to coat. Serve the steak slices fanned on a bed of good basmati rice with lemon grilled zucchini (see recipe in Chapter 1).

Cold Shrimp and Noodle Salad

1 cup	bottled Italian dressing (low-cal if you prefer)	250 ml
1/2 cup	Asian fish sauce	125 ml
1	2-inch/5-cm piece of fresh ginger, peeled and finely diced	1
1	bunch fresh basil, washed with stems removed and torn into strips	1
Approximately 1 1/2 lb	large shrimp, cooked and peeled	675 g
Approximately 1 lb	Asian noodles	450 g
1	12 oz/350 ml can water chestnuts, drained and cut into thirds	1
1/2	red or yellow pepper, halved again and cut into long strips	1/2
1/2	English cucumber, skin on, seeded, and sliced into long thin strips	1/2

1 Combine the dressing, fish sauce, ginger, and half the basil in a large bowl. Add the shrimp and toss to mix well. Set aside to marinate for 30 minutes.
2 Bring a large pot of water to boil over high heat and add the noodles. Cook the noodles for 1 to 2 minutes or until al dente.
3 Drain the noodles immediately and rinse them under cold water to stop them from cooking. Drain again once they've cooled off.
4 Add the noodles, water chestnuts, peppers, and cucumber to the shrimp. Toss to coat everything in the dressing.
5 Serve the salad with remaining basil as a garnish.

You can also serve this one as a light main course on one of those hot August nights (with apologies to Neil Diamond). We use bottled Italian dressing for a certain *je ne sais quoi*, but you can easily substitute your own oil and vinegar dressing if you want. You can get the fish sauce (called nam pla) and the Asian noodles (called somen) at any Asian grocery store, as well as at many mainstream supermarkets. You can also use an equal amount of vermicelli instead of the Asian noodles, as they're basically the same thing and are cooked the same way for the same amount of time. If you can't get your hands on water chestnuts, toss in a handful of roasted peanuts or sunflower seeds just before serving for a nice crunch.

Serves 6 as an appetizer

The Most Perfect Meal Ever Made

"Poultry is for the cook what canvas is for the painter."
Jean Anthelme Brillat-Savarin

Over the course of shooting *The Great Canadian Food Show* we have had the pleasure of sharing a glass or two with many a wonderful food lover. Usually it's at the end of a long day of filming, while sitting around at the back of a restaurant or on a porch, sipping a drink and trading food stories. We've met great chefs, accomplished cooks, and enthusiastic amateurs. All speak of food and cooking with a tremble of joy and passion in their voices. The most memorable meal, the worst disaster, the most unusual condiment, the big save when everything was falling apart . . . you know what we mean. Sooner or later, the conversation usually turns to what everyone cooks when they're at home. Overwhelmingly, the single most beloved dinner is the exquisitely simple roast chicken with all the fixings: stuffing, mashed potatoes, veggies, and gravy.

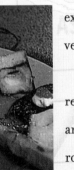

Unlike the big holiday production starring Tom Turkey, a roast chicken is a relatively simple affair . . . sort of a smaller off-Broadway run. Stick it in the oven and an hour and a half later . . . presto, bingo, bango! A delicious gourmet meal! A roasted chicken is more than the sum of its parts. Sure, there's lots you can do with a chicken breast or a leg or a thigh, but only by slowly roasting the entire bird intact can you get that singular homemade, comfort food, feel-good, Walton Mountain taste and aroma. And what an aroma! It insinuates itself into your very soul. It's a smell that reminds you that everything is good and right in the world. Roast a chicken and people start hugging each other.

There are many types of birds one can roast. From squab to game hen, from capon to free range. As it is a simple recipe, you owe it to yourself to get the best bird you can find. The skin of a chicken is nature's cooking vessel and, once done, its crispy crackling self can be left aside by those who have the fortitude to resist its siren call. Never buy anything less than grade A, and give a free-range bird a try — it's worth the few extra bucks. When purchasing your bird, it should be free of feathers or prickly things and the skin should be completely intact. If it is pre-wrapped, as in most commercial supermarkets, always check the wrapping date on the label. If it's more than two days old, move on.

Here are three recipes for the roasted bird. The Basic Bird recipe includes our secret step to the juiciest chicken every time. Enjoy and experiment. Keith Richards once said something like, "There's only one song ever written and every other song is just a variation on that theme." It's the same for the roasted chicken. Once you get the basics down pat, there are any number of different preparations, stuffings, sauces, and seasonings you can try. Go crazy; knock yourself out.

Please note that we have not included recipes for stuffing. We're saving that for our next book (the working title is *Carlo Does a Turkey*). Remember that if you're going to stuff your chicken it will alter the cooking time. Our tip here is to insert the handle of a teaspoon through the cavity and into the middle of the stuffed bird. The spoon will act as a heat conductor and cook the stuffing from the inside out.

The Basic Bird

4 1/2 lbs	chicken (fresh)	2 kg	**Serves 2 easily and 4 with lots of side dishes**
2 quarts	water	2 L	
4 tbsp	salt	60 ml	
2 tsp	sugar	10 ml	
1	lemon, halved	1	
2	garlic cloves, diced	2	
2	sprigs each thyme, savory, rosemary, and tarragon (or 2 tsp/10 ml each dried)	2	
2 tbsp	butter, softened	30 ml	
	Salt and freshly cracked pepper		

1 Wash the chicken inside and out under cold running water. Pat dry.
2 Pour water into a large soup pot and add the salt and sugar while stirring until they dissolve. You have now made a brine mixture.
3 Immerse your bird in the brine and let it soak for half an hour. Remove from the water and pat the chicken dry (inside and out).

4 Preheat your oven to 375°F (190°C).

5 Squeeze lemon juice into the chicken's cavity. Toss in the lemons and then the garlic and half the herbs.

6 Mix the remaining herbs with the butter in a small bowl. Gently separate the skin from the breast meat (use your fingers and make sure not to tear the skin). Slide the butter and herb mixture under the skin.

7 Gently truss your bird. Season with salt and fresh cracked pepper.

8 Place the chicken on a rack in the roasting pan and place in the centre of the oven with the breasts facing towards the back.

9 Roast for about 1 hour and 20 minutes, or until the juices run clear and the leg can be easily pulled away with a little tug. After the first hour, make sure you baste generously with the pan drippings every 7 minutes or so to get that great crackled skin.

10 Remove the chicken from the pan and tent with tin foil for at least 15 minutes before serving to allow the juices to settle. Congratulations, you have now made one of the single greatest meals ever.

11 Serve with your favourite side dishes and gravy (see recipe at the end of this chapter).

The Spicy Bird

This is a spicy-tangy recipe that uses a variation on an ages-old Portuguese piri piri sauce, which should be made a few hours in advance so that the flavours can blend properly. If you can't find Scotch bonnet chilies, substitute the hottest chilies you can get your hands on.

Serves 2 easily and 4 with lots of side dishes

2	garlic cloves, diced	2
3	Scotch bonnet chilies, seeded and diced	3
1/3 cup	red wine vinegar	75 ml
1 cup	olive oil	250 ml
8	bay leaves	8
	Salt and freshly cracked pepper, to taste	
4 1/2 lbs	chicken, brine-soaked as in the Basic Bird recipe	2 kg

1 Combine the garlic, chilies, vinegar, and ¾ of the olive oil in a jar and shake to mix. Let stand at room temperature for at least 2 hours.

2 Preheat your oven to 375°F (190°C).

3 Purée the bay leaves with the remaining olive oil, salt, and fresh cracked pepper to taste. Rub the chicken inside and out with the bay leaf oil.

4 Rub the outside with about ⅓ of the hot sauce.
5 Roast for about 1 hour and 20 minutes, or until the juices run clear and the leg can be easily pulled away with a little tug. After the first hour, make sure you baste generously with the hot sauce every 7 minutes or so.
6 Remove the chicken from the pan and tent with tin foil for at least 15 minutes before serving to allow the juices to settle.

The Ultimate Bird

1	black truffle	1
1	lemon, halved	1
4 ½ lbs	chicken, brine-soaked as in the Basic Bird recipe	2 kg
2	sprigs each thyme, savory, rosemary, and tarragon (or 2 tsp/10 ml each dried)	2
2	garlic cloves, diced	2
3	shallots, diced	3
2 tbsp	butter, softened	30 ml
	Salt and freshly cracked pepper	
4	bacon strips	4

1 Preheat your oven to 375°F (190°C).
2 Slice the truffle into 10 rounds.
3 Squeeze the lemon juice into the cavity of the chicken. Add the lemon halves, half of the herbs and garlic, and the shallots.
4 Mix the remaining herbs and garlic with the butter.
5 Carefully separate the skin from the chicken breasts and slather with the herb butter. Arrange truffle slices on the breasts between the skin and the butter.
6 Gently truss the bird. Season with salt and fresh cracked pepper. Lay the bacon strips over top of the chicken so as to cover the breasts.
7 Place the chicken on a rack in the roasting pan and roast in the middle of the oven with the breasts pointing towards the rear for about 1 hour and 20 minutes.
8 After roasting for 45 minutes, remove the bacon strips. Baste with lovely pan juices every 5 minutes during the last 20 minutes of the roasting process.

Warning: This recipe calls for truffles. Fresh truffles are possibly the single most expensive foodstuff in the world (at this writing, the black version was going for around $2000 per kilogram). There are two reasons for the expense: First, truffles grow only in small regions of France and Italy (although we hear there is a guy in Oregon trying to grow them) and only in the root system of certain oak trees. Second, in the days of Escoffier, the French put truffles on everything...cornflakes, cheesecake, burritos, you name it! Those darned French gourmands ate their way through most of the wild truffle caches! Obviously this is one of those special-occasion treats. We recommend the small black truffles in oil that are available at most specialty food stores for under $30, or the truffle oil itself, which you can combine with the butter that goes under the skin. Either way, this is one incredibly intense taste experience.

Serves 2

9 Tent the chicken with tin foil for 15 minutes before serving so that the juices settle.

10 Carefully slice the entire breast away from the carcass as one big piece so that the skin and truffles remain with the breast. Serve immediately with gravy and favourite side dishes.

Gravy

Your chicken should have come with the giblets in a small bag stuffed into the cavity. The giblets are the neck, liver, heart, and gizzard (lower stomach) of the bird, and while not particularly appetizing themselves, they are chock full of flavour for your gravy.

The secret to no-lump gravy is using a roux instead of dumping the flour right into the liquid. There's just one thing you have to remember with the roux: Don't overcook the flour! In order to get that deep brown colour and a lovely nutty taste, you have to cook the flour deeply without overheating and burning it. This process will also reduce the flour's thickening power by as much as 75 percent. Use a heavy-bottomed frying pan or cast-iron skillet for best results.

Makes 2 cups of gravy

1	package giblets, chopped	1
1	bay leaf	1
1/2	small onion, diced	1/2
2 cups	cold water	500 ml
	Drippings from chicken's roasting pan	
1/2 cup	white wine	125 ml
2 tbsp	roux	30 ml
	Salt and freshly cracked pepper	
2 tbsp	chopped fresh parsley	30 ml

1 In a medium saucepan, add the giblets, bay leaf, and onion to the cold water. Bring to a boil and reduce heat to simmer for about half an hour. Strain the liquid through a sieve and reserve.

2 Pour the drippings from the chicken's roasting pan into a measuring cup. Let it settle and spoon off all but 3 tbsp (45 ml) of the fat floating on top of the pan juices.

3 Place the roasting pan on the stove-top over a medium-high heat. Add the white wine and deglaze the pan, scraping up all the juicy brown bits clinging to the bottom, until the wine is almost gone.

4 Pour in the giblet stock and reserved pan drippings. Bring to a boil.

5 Remove the roasting pan from the heat and pour its contents in a steady stream into the roux, whisking as you go, over a high heat.

6 Reduce heat to medium-low and season with salt and fresh cracked pepper. Stir in the parsley for colour and serve immediately.

Roux

4 tbsp	flour	60 ml
4 tbsp	unsalted butter	60 ml

1 In a heavy-bottomed sauce pan, melt the butter over a medium heat and add the flour, stirring until well mixed.

2 Cook for 8 to 10 minutes or until a golden-brown paste has formed.

The Perogie Ladies of Kamsack, Saskatchewan

Consider the humble perogie (pronounced "pero-hay" in the original Polish, *verennky* in Ukrainian, thank you very much). Cousin to the more celebrated gnocchi, this delectable little orb is a two-starch regular in your average Canadian Prairie diet. Inexpensive and easy to make, perogies kept many families alive during the harsh Canadian winters of the 1930s, when there was little else to eat. Today, the fabled perogie has gone from survival staple to popular comfort food. These potato-stuffed dumplings are to Saskatchewan what bar-b-que is to Kansas City, and every small community dotted across these vast flatlands takes their perogie-making big time serious. And nowhere more so than in Kamsack, population 2200.

Kamsack, Saskatchewan, is about 200 miles northeast of Regina (if you're going to overnight in Kamsack, I'd suggest the Duck Mountain Motel), in the heart of wheat and potatoes country. It's your typical small Prairie town where family and community are still valued above all else. It is a place with more churches than restaurants. Take Queen Elizabeth Boulevard and hang a left at the Elks Hall and you'll come upon the Ukrainian-Catholic hall and perogie world headquarters for Anna Rosowsky, Stella Matzala, and the other 20 or so Perogie Ladies of Kamsack.

Every Tuesday morning, the ladies get together and hand-make some 100 dozen perogies for sale in support of their church. Over the years they've raised in excess of $100,000, selling their boiled treasures far and wide at $1.25 a dozen. That's a lot of perogies. Admission to their inner sanctum isn't free; you have to earn your way in, so be prepared to roll up your sleeves, roll out the dough, and commence fillin'. They use empty soup cans to cut perfect circles from the homemade dough, and then stuff and pinch each little packet by hand (a few years ago the local baker donated his dough mixer when he retired; before that they made the dough by hand). The potato stuffing is mixed with onion, sour cream, cabbage, or Cheez Whiz – a decidedly Canadian variation. The perogies are then boiled, frozen, and bagged for sale.

Perogie-making is more than a fundraising venture for these ladies. They sit at long tables stuffing and pinching, chatting and laughing. Most of these women are in their mid-sixties to mid-eighties. Several generations of family drop in to say hello over the course of the day. There's always a pot of tea on the stove and usually a local Ukrainian musician comes in to play tunes from the old country. An enviable warmth and closeness permeates the hall. This palpable sense of community and celebration is the true blessing food brings when shared with others. Be good to yourself: Eat a perogie.

Perogies with Three Fillings

Here is the recipe for perogie dough and a number of fillings as offered by Marg Ratushny and Anna Rosowsky of the St. Josaphat's Ukrainian Catholic Women's League of Kamsack, Saskatchewan.

Makes approximately 2 dozen perogies

Perogie Dough

4 cups	all-purpose flour	1 L
1 tsp	salt	5 ml
1/2 cup	melted margarine	125 ml
1	egg, beaten	1
1 1/2 cups	warm water	375 ml

1 Mix and knead all the ingredients together to form a soft dough.
2 Let sit at room temperature for 2 hours.

Mushroom Filling

2 tbsp	vegetable oil	30 ml
1	medium onion, chopped	1
2	10-oz/300 ml cans drained and ground mushrooms (or 2 cups/500 ml chopped fresh mushrooms)	2
1 tbsp	bread crumbs	15 ml

1 Heat oil in a skillet over medium-high heat.
2 Add onion. Reduce heat to medium and sauté until golden brown.
3 Add remaining ingredients and mix well. Continue to sauté for 2 minutes. Allow the mixture to cool before spooning onto the perogie dough.

Cottage Cheese Filling

2 cups	dry cottage cheese, drained	500 ml
1	egg, beaten	1
	Salt, to taste	

Combine all the ingredients and mix well. An additional egg or some sour cream may be added if the cottage cheese is too dry.

Sauerkraut Filling

3 cups	sauerkraut	750 ml
4 tbsp	unsalted butter	60 ml
1	medium onion, chopped	1
	Salt and freshly cracked pepper, to taste	

1 Rinse sauerkraut in warm water, squeeze, and chop finely.
2 Meanwhile, melt butter in a skillet over a medium-high heat. Add onion and reduce heat to medium. Cook until onion is translucent.
3 Add sauerkraut, salt, and freshly cracked pepper to taste and cook over a low heat for 15 minutes.
4 Be sure to allow the mixture to cool before assembling the perogies.

To assemble and cook the perogies:

1 Bring 3 quarts (3 L) of salted water to a gentle boil.
2 Roll out the dough on a floured surface to about ¼-in (0.5-cm) thickness.
3 Using a clean, empty soup can (10 oz/284 ml), cut out circles from the dough.
4 Place 1 tsp (5 ml) of filling in the middle of each round.
5 Fold the dough over and pinch the edges to form half moons.
6 Drop the perogies into the boiling water a few at a time and cook for 3 to 4 minutes, or until they rise to the surface.
7 Drain in a colander, rinsing with cold water.

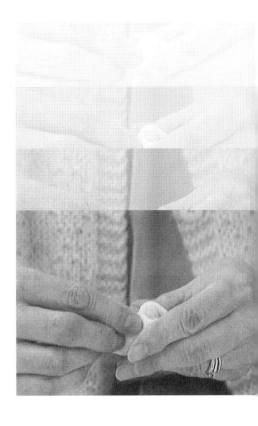

The Best Ever Meat Loaf

The ultimate comfort food from a recipe by Eleanor Chernoff in memory of Jennie Schebywolok.

Serves 6 with mashed potatoes, string beans, and gravy

2	eggs, beaten	2
2/3 cup	2% milk	150 ml
2 tsp	salt	10 ml
1/4 tsp	freshly cracked pepper	1 ml
3	slices bread, toasted and processed into crumbs	3
1	medium onion, diced	1
1/2 cup	shredded carrot	125 ml
1 cup	grated cheese (mozzarella or cheddar)	250 ml
Approximately 1 2/3 lb	ground beef	750 g
4 tbsp	brown sugar	60 ml
4 tbsp	ketchup	60 ml
1 tbsp	prepared mustard	15 ml

1 Preheat your oven to 350°F (180°C).
2 In a large bowl, mix eggs, milk, salt, pepper, and bread crumbs together.
3 Add the onion, carrot, cheese, and ground beef. Mix well.
4 Pour the mixture into a glass casserole dish and pack down evenly.
5 In a small bowl, combine the brown sugar, ketchup, and mustard. Spread the mixture evenly over the top of the meat loaf.
6 Bake in the middle of the oven for 1 hour. Let sit for 10 minutes before serving.

Cabbage Bean Soup

Thanks to Anne Maksymetz for this one.

Serves 6

3 tbsp	vegetable oil	45 ml
1	large onion, chopped	1
2	garlic cloves, minced	2
3 cups	coarsely shredded cabbage	750 ml
3 cups	beef stock	750 ml
3 cups	water	750 ml
1 tsp	dried oregano	5 ml
	Salt and freshly cracked pepper, to taste	
2	14-oz/398 ml cans of white kidney beans, rinsed and drained	2
2	frankfurters, sliced	2

1 Heat oil in a soup pot over a medium-high heat. Add onion and garlic and sauté for 5 minutes, being sure not to burn the garlic.
2 Stir in the cabbage and sauté for 5 minutes.
3 Add the stock, water, oregano, salt, and fresh cracked pepper. Cover and simmer for 25 minutes.
4 Add the beans and frankfurters and simmer for 5 minutes longer.
5 Serve with a good loaf of crusty bread and unsalted butter.

Variations on the theme: Instead of frankfurters consider using smoked sausage (like kielbasa) or slices of brisket. There are many different types of canned beans to experiment with, including a nice five-bean mixture. While cabbage is the backbone of the soup, try replacing half of it with kale, dandelion greens, or spinach. If you do replace the cabbage with another less-hardy green, be sure to add them at the end with the beans. They'll get all mushy if you put them in at the same time as the big hearty cabbage.

Five-Minute Fudge

3/4 cup	evaporated milk	175 ml
1 1/4 cups	white sugar	300 ml
1/4 tsp	salt	1 ml
1 1/2 cups	miniature marshmallows	375 ml
1/2 cup	walnuts, coarsely chopped	125 ml
1 1/2 cups	semi-sweet chocolate chips	375 ml
1 tsp	vanilla	5 ml

Here's an instant sugar fix guaranteed to send you into a diabetic coma, courtesy of Mary Kindiak. She says you can store the fudge in a sealed container in the fridge. Yeah, right . . . as if these goodies are ever going to last that long!

Makes about 2 lbs / 1 kg

1 Mix the evaporated milk, sugar, and salt together in a large saucepan over a medium-high heat.
2 Bring to a boil and reduce heat to medium, simmering for 5 minutes and stirring constantly to make sure the sugar dissolves completely.
3 Remove from heat when the mixture begins to bubble anew around the sides of the pan.
4 Add the remaining ingredients. Stir the fudge mixture until the marshmallows and chocolate have melted completely.
5 Pour the fudge into a buttered 8-inch/20-cm square pan and cool. Cut into squares and enjoy.

Poppy Seed Cake

As suggested by Arlene Tataryn.

Makes one cake

For the cake:

4 tbsp	poppy seeds	60 ml
4 tbsp	2% milk	60 ml
1	lemon supreme cake mix	1
1	3-oz/85-g package of instant banana pudding	1
4	eggs, beaten	4
1/2 cup	vegetable oil	125 ml
1 cup	warm water	250 ml

For the spice mixture:

1 tbsp	cocoa	15 ml
1 tbsp	cinnamon	15 ml
1 tbsp	sugar	15 ml

For the glaze:

3 tbsp	freshly squeezed lemon juice	45 ml
6 tbsp	white sugar	90 ml

1 Soak the poppy seeds overnight in the milk.
2 Preheat your oven to 350°F (180°C).
3 Combine the cake mix, pudding, eggs, oil, and water and mix well. Add the poppy seeds and milk and continue to mix.
4 Grease and lightly flour a bundt pan.
5 Pour one-third of the cake mixture into the pan. Sprinkle one-third of the spice mixture over top. Repeat until all of the cake and spice mixture are used.
6 Bake the cake in the middle of the oven for 1 hour.
7 Meanwhile, in a small saucepan, bring the lemon juice to a gentle boil over a medium-high heat. Add the sugar and stir until completely dissolved. Simmer for 2 minutes longer.
8 Once baked, turn the cake over onto a plate and drizzle with the glaze.

The Wild Mushroom Hunt

We were in the Bugaboo Mountains of British Columbia shooting the heli-hiking episode when word reached us by radio phone that things were not looking good mushroom-wise in the Gatineau Hills of Quebec, which was the next stop on our shooting schedule. It seems there had been a lot of rain of late in them thar hills and the fungi were nowhere to be found. While mushrooms thrive in damp, moist places, they are not precipitationally inclined. No mushrooms, no story.

Cancelling a shoot is a big deal. The story had been set out months in advance, crews had been booked, and we were to fly in from Calgary two days hence to hunt for wild porcini mushrooms with a band of avid mycologists.

There is always one temperamental diva on every shoot. In our case, it is Mother Nature. At one point we were set to spend several days out on the Atlantic Ocean to harpoon giant bluefin tuna for the Japanese sushi market. Harpooning a tuna ain't easy, but it kills the fish quickly, meaning adrenalin is not released into the bloodstream, meaning the prized succulent meat is more tender and flavourful. The Japanese pay a huge premium for this delicacy, as it is flash-frozen and shipped to Japan within 24 hours of being caught. We waited for weeks for the call that the tuna were running. A crew was on standby ready to fly out to the coast on a day's notice. Alas, by the time the tuna showed up our schedule had been set and we had to pass on the story.

On another occasion, we were going to do a piece about the storied Fuji apple from the Okanagan Valley of British Columbia. Three weeks before the shoot, a freak hailstorm swept across the valley and wiped out most of the apple crop. No more story. These are the perils of shooting an entire 13-episode series in the field.

The irony is that the Bugaboos were fairly bursting with all manner of wild fungi ready to be picked. For a brief moment we considered "transplanting" the shrooms from B.C. to the Gatineau Hills, but we realized such dastardly subterfuge would violate the spirit of the show. In the end the skies parted and the sun and the mushrooms came out as we journeyed east.

Next to wine, mushrooms are probably the most taste-complex ingredient one can add to a dish. They are pungent and musky, and simply sautéing them will release a deep rich taste that will raise your sauces and soups to new heights. Grind up a dried wild mushroom and sprinkle it on a simple pasta dish for a *je ne sais quoi* whoop-de-do that will have you and yours going back for seconds. Fresh porcini or morels are usually unavailable to most of us non-professional mere-mortal cooks, so the dried variety is the next best thing. In fact, dried mushrooms are actually better when reconstituted in sauces, soups, and stocks.

Chicken Breasts Stuffed with Wild Mushrooms and Porcini Butter

This is a super-easy main course employing the magic of the shroom for maximum taste. Use Parmesan Reggiano for the best results, and the amount of garlic can vary quite a bit depending on your love of the stinking rose.

Serves 6 as a main course

1 oz	dried wild mushrooms (such as porcini or morel)	30 g
8	half chicken breasts, deboned and skin removed	8
6 oz	Parmesan cheese, grated (preferably Parmesan Reggiano)	170 g
1/2	bunch fresh parsley, chopped with stems removed	1/2
6	garlic cloves, diced	6
1/2 tsp	dried sage	2 ml
2	eggs, beaten	2
	Salt and freshly cracked pepper	
8 tbsp	unsalted butter	120 ml
	Flour (for dredging)	

1 Reconstitute the wild mushrooms by soaking them for 30 minutes in 1 cup (250 ml) of boiling water. Strain and chop the mushrooms. Be sure to reserve the now-musky deep brown soaking liquid to make the accompanying sauce.

2 Coarsely chop 2 of the chicken breasts and place in a food processor along with the mushrooms, cheese, parsley, garlic, sage, and eggs. Pulse the mixture several times until mixture is well chopped. Add salt and fresh cracked pepper.

3 Place a sheet of plastic wrap on a cutting board or work surface. Place a chicken breast on top, then cover it with another sheet of plastic wrap. Pound the chicken breast until it is an even ⅓-inch (0.75-cm) thickness. Repeat the procedure with the other chicken breasts.

4 Place a flattened chicken breast on the work surface and season with salt and freshly cracked pepper. Spoon one-sixth of the filling onto the side of the chicken breast closest to you, leaving a ¼-inch (0.5-cm) border on the sides. Roll the chicken breast away from you like a big poultry spring roll wrapper and secure with 2 toothpicks. Repeat with the other chicken breasts.

5 Melt 2 tbsp (30 ml) of the butter in a large skillet over a medium-high heat. Lightly dredge the chicken breasts in flour, being sure to shake off any excess. Sauté 3 of the chicken breasts for 5 minutes per side until a nice crispy brown exterior is achieved. Remove the chicken breasts and repeat with the other 3.

6 Return the first 3 chicken breasts to the skillet and cover. Reduce the heat to medium and cook for another 15 minutes, turning the chicken breasts once. Remove the chicken breasts and set aside, covered in tin foil to keep warm.

7 Return the heat to medium-high and add the reserved porcini liquid to deglaze the pan. Bring to a gentle boil and scrape up all the nice juicy brown bits. Continue to gently boil until the liquid is reduced to a few spoonfuls. The mushroom flavour will now have intensified in this precious reduction. Add the remaining butter and turn the heat down to low. Whisk the butter until it melts. Season with salt and fresh cracked pepper.

8 Plate 1 chicken breast per person and drizzle the porcini butter over top. Serve with risotto.

Never Wash a Mushroom

Shrooms are extremely porous fungi that absorb water like a sponge. The water is then released into the pan when cooked, rendering the mushrooms mushy and their taste diluted. Blah. We've found that the best way to clean dirt from mushrooms is to use a toothbrush (preferably a new one!) or paper towel.

Wild Mushroom and Goat Cheese Omelette

Most grocery stores now carry a selection of goat cheese, including some flavoured with a mix of peppers or sun-dried tomatoes, which gives you a ready-made opportunity to experiment. Make sure that the cheese is at room temperature before starting this recipe or it will be difficult to mix with the mushrooms and will interfere with the cooking process of the eggs.

Serves 6 as a great brunch or light dinner

6 tbsp	unsalted butter	90 ml
3/4 lb	assorted mushrooms (shiitake, portobello, morel, etc.) cleaned, sliced, and stems discarded	350 g
1/2	white onion, thinly sliced	1/2
1/2	red pepper, thinly sliced with white pulpy flesh removed	1/2
6	garlic cloves, coarsely diced	6
1 tbsp	dried sage	15 ml
1 lb	goat cheese (3 packets)	450 g
	Salt and freshly cracked pepper	
18	large eggs	18
1/2	bunch fresh parsley, coarsely chopped and stems discarded	1/2

1 Preheat your oven to 300°F (150°C).

2 Melt 3 tbsp (45 ml) of the unsalted butter in a medium non-stick skillet over a medium-high heat. Add the mushrooms, onion, red pepper, garlic, and sage. Reduce heat to medium and sauté for about 5 minutes. Pour yourself another cup of coffee.

3 Transfer the mushroom mixture to a large bowl and fold in the goat cheese until you get a nice gooey consistency. Season with salt and fresh cracked pepper.

4 In another bowl combine the eggs and parsley. Beat the eggs until well blended. Season with salt and fresh cracked pepper.

5 Melt ½ tbsp (7 ml) of butter over medium-high heat in the same non-stick skillet in which you sautéed the mushrooms until the butter begins to foam.

6 Pour in one-sixth of the egg mixture and swirl the skillet to evenly distribute the egg about the pan. The underside of the omelette will begin to cook first, while the top will remain liquid. Continue to cook until the omelette is set and the edges can be lifted carefully with a spatula.

7 Place one-sixth of the mushroom and cheese mixture in the middle of the omelette. Be careful not to mound it too high. If you try to spread it around a bit, be careful not to tear the omelette underneath, otherwise you'll have a big cheesy leak on your hands.

8 Fold the omelette over and let it cook for a bit longer until the egg mixture adheres to itself and envelops the mushrooms and cheese mixture.

9 Slide the omelette onto a baking sheet and tent with tin foil. Stick the baking sheet in the oven and repeat the cooking process until you have yourself 6 delicious omelettes.

10 Serve with toasted crusty bread, pan-fried or grilled tomato halves, and a nice side salad or melon slices.

Lamb Shanks with Root Veggies, Mushrooms, and Gremolata

For the lamb:

1/4 cup	dried porcini mushrooms	50 g
3 cups	water	750 ml
4 tbsp	olive oil	60 ml
4 tbsp	unsalted butter	60 ml
4	leeks, white parts only, coarsely chopped, then washed	4
4	garlic cloves, finely chopped	4
2	sprigs fresh rosemary	2
2	bay leaves	2
3	large portobello mushrooms, stems discarded, halved, then sliced	3
3	potatoes, peeled and quartered	3
2	sweet potatoes, peeled and chopped into 1/2-inch/1-cm slices	2
3	parsnips, peeled and chopped into 1/2-inch/1-cm slices	3
6	big juicy lamb shanks (or 12 if they're small; use your judgement)	6
	Salt and freshly cracked pepper	
	Flour (for dredging)	
3 cups	white wine	750 ml
3 cups	beef stock	750 ml
	Juice of 1 lemon	
2 tbsp	tomato paste	30 ml
Approximately 1 lb	frozen baby peas	450 g
3	carrots, peeled and finely diced	3

This rather inexpensive cut of meat becomes an incredibly profound melt-in-your-mouth taste treat thanks to a slow braising process. The lamb meat falls away from the bone and rests gently on your fork. If lamb is not your thing, substitute veal shanks. Both are available at any reputable butcher.

Serves 6 as a main course

For the gremolata:

6 tbsp	coarsely chopped parsley	90 ml
2 tbsp	finely diced lemon peel	30 ml
1	garlic clove, finely diced	1

1 For the gremolata, combine the parsley, lemon peel, and garlic in a small bowl and set aside.

2 Place the porcini mushrooms in a microwave-proof bowl with the water and cover with plastic wrap, pushing down so that the shrooms are submerged. Nuke for 5 minutes on high and set aside for 15 minutes. Drain the liquid through a fine sieve into a container. Set the liquid aside and finely dice the reconstituted porcini.

3 Preheat your oven to 350°F (180°C).

4 Heat half the olive oil and butter in a large ovenproof pot over medium-high heat until the butter begins to foam. Add the leeks, garlic, rosemary, and bay leaves. Reduce the heat and sauté for 10 minutes or so, stirring now and then. Add the porcini and portobello mushrooms, potatoes, sweet potatoes, and parsnips and toss so that everything is well coated. Sauté for another 5 or 6 minutes.

5 Combine the remaining butter and olive oil in a large skillet over a medium-high heat until the butter begins to foam.

6 Season the lamb shanks with salt and fresh cracked pepper and dredge them in the flour, shaking off any excess. Brown the shanks 3 or 4 at a time until nicely browned, about 3 or 4 minutes per side. As you finish browning each batch, transfer the shanks to the pot and sit them on top of the veggies. Repeat with the remaining shanks until all are done.

7 Add the wine to the skillet and increase the heat to high. Once the wine begins to bubble, use a wooden spoon to scrape up all the delicious juicy brown bits from the bottom and sides of the skillet. Bubble away for 5 minutes and pour the wine reduction into the pot.

8 Add the porcini broth, beef stock, and lemon juice to the pot. Bring the whole thing to a boil and cover. Place the pot in the middle of the oven and bake for 1 hour. Remove the lid from the pot and continue to bake for another 45 minutes.

9 Remove the pot from the oven and add the tomato paste, peas, and carrots. Stir well and cover again. Let the pot sit for 10 minutes.

10 To serve, place 1 shank in the middle of each serving plate using tongs. Surround the shanks with the veggies and spoon the wonderfully rich broth over top. Sprinkle the gremolata on top and serve immediately. Delicioso.

Lamb with Lemon Grilled Zucchini

Bar-b-qued Pineapple

Confit de Canard *and* Pommes à l'Ail

Tartare aux Deux Saumons

Grilled Sea Bass with
Watermelon-Mango Salsa

Perogies

The Fabled Maritime Lobster Roll

Baby Spinach and Mushroom Salad

The Mighty Digby Scallop

The Digby sea scallop. Possibly the plumpest, juiciest bivalve in all the world. It is the sirloin of seafood, the scallop with a wallop. Pan-fried till crispy brown and caramelized on either side, warm and opaque in the middle, the Digby scallop is an exquisite taste sensation unlike any other shellfish. And until recently, it's a taste you've probably never had the chance to experience.

When you think scallop, you likely think of a gelatinous marshmallow-like blob that is not so much white as lacking any appreciable colour, let alone texture. It is gooey and slimy and has a mild seafood flavour. This pale pretender is to a real scallop what a slice of white bread is to a seven-grain baguette.

A real, honest sea scallop is a wondrous thing. Its natural colour ranges from a soft pinkish-yellow to a beautiful orangey-brown. It sits up proud and firm like sirloin and has a profoundly unique taste that is at once mellow and complex. In fact, what you see at your local grocer or fishmonger is likely but the adductor muscle. The entire scallop (including the deliciously sweet roe) is eaten as you would a clam or mussel and is common in Europe. But it is also a smelly, temperamental little bugger, and therein lies the problem.

The scallops that you and I usually get are pre-shucked at a processing plant and then soaked in a phosphate bath. This process plumps the scallop full of water and bleaches away its natural colour, all the while rendering it odourless in deference to the once-delicate North American palate and sensibilities. If you've ever tried to pan-fry one of these chemically altered bivalves, chances are it has given up an unappetizing milky liquid as it sloshes about the pan without hope of reaching that golden brown colour you want. Alas, such an offering usually ends up chewy and overcooked. For this reason, most of us tend to favour the small bay scallop in salads or chowders. These little nibbles are delicate and sweet, but too small to be prepared in a manner befitting their larger sea-dwelling cousin.

But all is not lost, fellow scallopini, for in recent years quality fishmongers (see Chapter 19) have taken to stocking the real article when it's in season. An unadulterated scallop, known in the business as a "dry scallop," costs a few bucks more per kilogram, but is well worth the price in texture and taste. Do yourself a favour and buy a scallop that tastes better than the container it comes in.

As for Digby, Nova Scotia, let's just say that it is the prototypical Maritime fishing village. Pulling into the harbour after a long drive and ferry ride, stretching our travel-weary bones, we inhaled deeply those first heady lungfuls of sweet salt air so intoxicating to a landlubber, to someone "from away." There are thousands of small fishing villages up and down the coast of Atlantic Canada that look almost exactly like Digby. Lucky us. This is a working town. Picturesque, yes. Requisite tourist shops line the main drag, shilling driftwood art and hand-carved statues of bearded fishermen in sou'westers and wellies smoking corncob pipes and staring off into the distance. But down in the harbour, scallop-draggers are tied up three abreast waiting to go to work, crewed by men who have no romantic illusions about the sea.

These are hard-working people whose livelihood has long been dictated by the vagaries of international finance and regulatory bodies that affect the price of their catch. You ain't gonna get rich as a scallop fisher-man, but you can make a comfortable living at it. And what a place to work every day! Most of these guys, like Brian Longmire, whom we featured in the show, have now banded together and formed cooperatives, as there is always strength in numbers. There is long-term planning afoot, with money being put into aquaculture processes to ensure the sea scallop does not go the way of Atlantic cod. Moored over the scallop beds, we dined that sunny July afternoon on freshly shucked raw scallops as the gulls swooped and cackled overhead. The lads laughed and joked about being on national television, one of them apparently having shaved that morning for the first time in recent memory.

Later, we made our way up the hill from the harbour to The Pines resort for a scallop-fest as prepared by Chef Claude Au'Coin. Chef Au'Coin has worked in some of the best kitchens from France to Bermuda, Switzerland to Philadelphia. But like all good Acadian sons, Claude came home to the Maritimes and now works his magic in the kitchens at The Pines. As celebrated wonderchefs go, Claude has his feet squarely on the ground. He's the kind of guy who'll come out from behind the big swinging doors and chat with you for a while over dinner.

The Pines itself is a wonderful resort sitting high on a bluff overlooking the harbour. It's actually run by the provincial government and is quite reasonably priced. One last thing: If you have occasion to stay there, consider one of the great little cottages they have out back. Our crew stayed in a couple of them on our visit to Digby. After a long day of shooting out on the water and in the sauna-like kitchens (we have to turn off the ventilation systems to preserve the audio when shooting in a commercial kitchen), it was a pleasure to sit out on the cottage porch surrounded by tall, aromatic pine trees. Feel the warm evening breeze on your face while nursing a fine single malt and watch the sun go down over the harbour below. A Maritime moment not available in any brochure.

Here are a few scallop recipes from Chef Claude Au'Coin's delectable repertoire. Enjoy.

Digby Scallop Mousse

Approximately 1 lb	fresh scallops	450 g
Pinch	each salt and white pepper	Pinch
2	egg whites	2
1	egg yolk	1
1/2 quart	35% cream	1/2 L

1 Preheat oven to 350°F (180°C).
2 Place scallops in a food processor and add salt and white pepper.
3 Purée scallops until smooth, occasionally scraping down the sides of the processor bowl with a spatula.
4 While processor is running on low setting, add egg whites and yolk one at a time.
5 Set processor on high and add the cream in a slow stream, again stopping occasionally to scrape down the sides of the bowl.
6 Pour the mousse mixture into 6 individual ramekins and set them in a roasting pan. Fill the pan with warm water until it reaches ¾ of the way up the side of the ramekins.
7 Bake in oven for 25 minutes, or until a toothpick comes out cleanly when inserted in the centres of the ramekins.

This is a very simple and elegant appetizer. The secret is to make sure all the ingredients are very cold before preparation. Once you get the hang of making this, try substituting other ingredients for the scallops (such as blanched asparagus, crabmeat, or smoked chicken). The mousse can be served warm or cold, depending on the time of year, and looks great on a bed of mixed greens that have been tossed with soy and flavoured vinegar.

Serves 6 as an appetizer

Grilled Scallops with Sun-Dried Tomato Sauce

You can also cook these scallops on the bar-b-que to get that nice grill marking on the white flesh. Just make sure the grill is lightly oiled and that you don't move them around once you've set them on the grill.

Serves 6 as a main course

1 cup	sun-dried tomatoes in olive oil	250 ml
3	garlic cloves, minced	3
3	shallots, chopped	3
3	medium plum tomatoes, seeded and diced	3
1 cup	dry red wine	250 ml
2 tbsp	balsamic vinegar	30 ml
1/2 tsp	cayenne pepper	2 ml
6	wooden skewers	6
36	large scallops	36
2 tbsp	olive oil	30 ml
	Salt, white pepper, and dried herbs	

For the sauce:
1. Strain the sun-dried tomatoes, reserving the oil.
2. Sauté the garlic and shallots in the reserved oil over medium-low heat until translucent, about 5 minutes.
3. Add tomatoes, red wine, vinegar, and cayenne pepper and simmer for 25 minutes.
4. Purée in a blender until smooth.
5. Strain into a saucepan and set aside. Add a little water if the sauce is too thick.

For the scallops:
1. Soak skewers in cold water for at least 1 hour.
2. Place 6 scallops on each skewer so that they are all lying flat.
3. Set your oven on broil (or your bar-b-que on medium-high).
4. Pat scallops dry and brush with a little olive oil.
5. Season the scallops with salt, white pepper, and any dried herb you might like.
6. Set under the broiler for 2 to 3 minutes per side, or until golden brown and opaque in the middle.
7. Remove scallops from skewers and plate immediately. Spoon sauce over scallops and serve.

In Search of a Canadian Cuisine

10

What exactly is "Canadian cuisine"? Is sushi made from Nova Scotia bluefin tuna any less Canuck than sugar pie featuring Quebec maple syrup? No. Canadian cuisine is as evolving and changing as the country is itself. Canadian cuisine is a fluid collision of world culinary influences and a wealth of fresh local ingredients.

To emphasize the point we took Carlo to the Ottawa Wine & Food Show, where he ate his way around the world. It was interesting to see smoked meat, wild boar, souvlaki, and dahl side by side. We've come a long way in these last few decades and our national culinary palate has now evolved to a sophisticated level where we are finally realizing that what's best to eat in the world is just up the road. Here are recipes from, or inspired by, some of the exhibitors we featured in that episode.

Cinnamon Crust Breast of Turkey with Sweet and Spicy Thai Cream Sauce

This is another recipe that calls for Thai chili paste. In our opinion, there is no substitute. Sure, there are other "heat agents" you can substitute, but no other condiment has the rich complexity of tastes packed into a teaspoonful. Thai chili sauce is available at any Asian market for a couple of bucks and will keep in your fridge door for months and months. An anglicized version (basically the same paste but with North American–type packaging for twice the price) is also available at many "mainstream" supermarkets.

Any butcher worth his apron strings will gladly sell you the turkey breasts alone, and lots of supermarkets now sell the big bird in parts. This is a little recipe we came up with that's sort of a Thai–Indian–Canuck combo-rama. You can substitute 6 half chicken breasts for the turkey if you like. Turkey, of course, is packed full of that natural hormone that makes one tired after digging in. The technical cooking term for that comfortable drowsiness is "the super dodo of love." Enjoy.

Serves 6 as a main course

5 tbsp	canola or other vegetable oil (for pan-frying)	75 ml
2	turkey breasts, trimmed and skin removed	2
	Salt and freshly cracked pepper, to taste	
4 tbsp	ground cinnamon	60 ml
6	garlic cloves, coarsely diced	6
6	shallots, coarsely diced	6
1 tsp	Thai chili paste	5 ml
2 cups	dry white wine	500 ml
1 3/4 cups	35% cream	425 ml
1/2 cup	pure maple syrup	125 ml
12	shiitake mushrooms, stems removed and coarsely chopped	12
1/2 cup	raisins or dried cranberries	125 ml
1/2 cup	almonds, slivered and toasted	125 ml
1/2 cup	baby sweet peas, fresh or frozen	125 ml

1 Preheat your oven to 350°F (180°C).
2 Heat 2 tbsp (30 ml) of the canola oil in a large skillet over a medium-high heat. Pat the turkey breasts dry with paper towel and season with salt, fresh cracked pepper, and the ground cinnamon.
3 Place one of the breasts into the skillet and fry until a nice dark brown cinnamon crust is created, about 3 or 4 minutes. Flip the breast and fry on the other side. Remove the breast to a medium baking pan. Add 2 more tbsp (30 ml) of oil to the skillet and reheat. Repeat the process with the second turkey breast, which you'll also remove to the baking pan and cover with tin foil.
4 Add the remaining oil to the skillet and heat. Add the garlic and shallots and then reduce the heat to medium so that the garlic doesn't burn. Sauté for 3 minutes. Add the Thai chili paste and stir until dissolved, about 30 seconds.
5 Bring the heat up to high. Count to 10 and pour in 1/2 cup (125 ml) of the white wine. It will bubble up immediately and you can begin deglazing the pan with a wooden spoon. Once you've scraped up all the nice brown bits that were clinging to the skillet, reduce the heat to medium-high and let the wine reduce to a mere couple of tablespoons. Add the remaining wine and the cream and bring to a boil.

6 Flip the tin foil off the turkey and pour in the sauce from the skillet. Turn the breasts over once or twice with tongs so that they're well coated. Re-tent with the tin foil and stick the baking pan in the oven for 30 minutes.

7 Remove the turkey breasts from the baking pan and set aside on a warming plate under the tin foil. Bring the sauce to a boil over a high heat and simmer for 5 minutes or so, until the sauce thickens a bit. Check the turkey breasts for accumulated juices. Add them to the sauce along with the maple syrup and mushrooms, and simmer for 2 minutes longer. Toss in the raisins, almonds, and peas and continue to simmer for a minute. Turn the heat down to low.

8 To serve, carve the turkey breasts against the grain into nice long slices. Fan the slices over a bed of basmati rice and drizzle the sauce over top. Make sure everybody gets some of the raisins, almonds, and peas. Serve with frosty cold beer.

Why You Should Sell Granny's Fancy-Shmancy China at Your Next Garage Sale

Any plate or bowl adorned with more than the simplest pattern is out. Solid colours, perhaps with a tiny detail or trim is *très* in. The food you cook and the time you put into presentation deserve more than a plate that competes for attention with your creation. Look at it this way: No one ever goes into the Louvre, walks up to the *Mona Lisa*, and says "Hey, nice frame!" The plate (or the bowl, for your wonderful soups) should be a simple canvas on which you posit your work of art for consumption.

Bar-b-qued Moose

1	moose, antlers removed	1
8 gallons	ketchup	30 L
5 1/2 gallons	Bob's moose marinating sauce	20 L
	Salt and freshly cracked pepper, to taste	
3 tbsp	dry mustard	45 ml
1	bay leaf	1
3	two-fours of fine Canadian beer	3

Our own recipe. No one else would take credit for it.

Serves 100 as a main course

1 Make sure the moose is dead.
2 Put moose on a skewer or in a very, very, very large skillet.
3 Cook over medium-high heat until done, about 9 days, basting occasionally with all the other ingredients, save and except for the beer.
4 Drink the beer.
5 Serve the moose with potatoes Anna and an asparagus soufflé.

Venison Shoulder Roast with Cranberry Cream Sauce

This works great with a nice veal shoulder roast if you can't get your hands on venison.

Serves 6 as a main course

2 1/4 lbs	venison shoulder roast, debunked and trimmed	1 kg
4	twigs fresh rosemary, petals removed and chopped	4
	Salt and freshly cracked pepper	
4 tbsp	unsalted butter	60 ml
1	small onion, finely chopped	1
10	juniper berries (or 2 tbsp/30 ml gin)	10
1/2 cup	good dry white wine	125 ml
4 tbsp	brandy	60 ml
2/3 cup	35% cream	150 ml
6 tbsp	cranberry jelly	90 ml

1 Preheat oven to 450°F (230°C).
2 Pat venison roast dry and rub with rosemary, salt, and fresh cracked pepper.
3 In a roasting pan, melt butter over medium-high heat until it begins to foam.
4 Add venison and brown on all sides until crispy brown and the rosemary has adhered to the roast.
5 Add onion and berries (or gin) to the pan and cook in the centre of the oven for 30 minutes.
6 After 30 minutes baste the roast in the pan drippings. Add wine to pan, reduce heat to 325°F (160°C), cover, and cook for 30 minutes.
7 Remove roast from pan and tent with tin foil to keep warm while the juices settle.
8 Place the pan on the stove-top at medium-high heat and deglaze with the brandy, scraping up all the juicy brown bits.
9 Add cream and cranberry jelly and reduce to desired consistency.
10 Serve with roasted potatoes and veggies.

Roast Goose with Two Stuffings

10 lbs	goose, cleaned, giblets reserved	5 kg
	Salt and freshly cracked pepper	
2 cups	white wine	500 ml
2 cups	water	500 ml
1 cup	apple cider	250 ml

1 Rinse the bird, inside and out, with cold water. Pat dry and prick the skin all over with a darning needle or a thick toothpick. Make sure you don't pierce the meat itself, just the skin, so that the goose juice doesn't get loose.

2 Season the inside of the bird with salt and freshly cracked pepper and truss the legs with kitchen twine.

3 Turn on 2 of your stove-top burners (front and back) to high.

4 Here's the fun part. Pour the wine, water, and cider into a large turkey roasting pan. Place 4 tea saucers or coffee mugs upside down in the pan. They should just clear the liquid. Now put a large plate on top of the cups. There's your handy-dandy goose-roasting platform!

5 Set the roasting pan on top of the burners and bring the liquid to a boil. Place the goose breast-side-down on the plate and cover (if your lid won't cover the bird, then tent with tin foil). Steam for 15 minutes. Reduce the heat to medium so that the liquid is gently simmering and continue to steam for 2 hours and 15 minutes, checking the liquid every now and then to make sure it's not all boiling away. In the meantime, watch *Babette's Feast* for inspiration. Set the goose aside to cool.

6 Once the bird is cool to the touch, preheat your oven to 350°F (180°C).

7 Undo the string on the front legs and loosely stuff the neck and chest cavities with the stuffing(s). Retruss the bird.

8 Place the goose breast-side-down on a rack in the same large roasting pan and cook for 30 minutes.

9 Flip the bird over and roast for another 30 minutes or until the skin is a nice crispy brown and juices run from the skin when pricked.

10 Let the goose rest for 15 minutes under tin foil before carving.

Another treat more common in "the Old Country" than over here is goose. A goose is a large noisy bird that deserves to get eaten. When properly cooked, its dark meat is extra tender and delicious with a slightly gamy taste (we mean that in a good way, folks!). The problem is that this honker is very greasy. We fix that by steaming the goose upside down in an oven over a bath of white wine and apple cider to draw out the fat before the traditional roasting process. Both of these stuffings can be baked inside the same goose cavity, but do extra on the stove-top.

The steaming liquid should be reserved and reduced for gravy, once you've spooned off the fat. The fat itself is wonderful for pan-frying potatoes...mmmm!

Serves 6 as a main course

Sausage Meat Stuffing

1 tbsp	unsalted butter	15 ml
2	medium onions, diced	2
2	celery stalks, diced	2
1 tbsp	dried savory	15 ml
1 tbsp	dried tarragon	15 ml
	Liver from the goose, finely diced	
1/2 lb	good fresh sausage meat, removed from casing	225 g
3	large tart apples (such as Granny Smith or Fuji), peeled, cored, and diced*	3
3/4 cup	bread crumbs	175 ml

* *Be sure to peel and core the apples at the last possible moment or they will go brown on you in no time.*

1 In a large skillet, melt butter over a medium heat. Add the onions and celery and cook until golden brown, about 8 to 10 minutes. Add savory and tarragon and cook a minute longer.
2 Add the liver and sausage meat and cook until browned.
3 Add apples and cook 5 minutes longer.
4 Transfer to a bowl, blend in bread crumbs, and let cool.

Sage and Onion Stuffing

3 tbsp	unsalted butter	45 ml
Approximately 1 lb	Spanish onions or white onions, finely chopped	450 g
3 tbsp	dried sage	45 ml
2	garlic cloves, diced	2
1 1/2 cups	bread crumbs	375 ml
1	egg, beaten	1
4 tbsp	35% cream	60 ml
	Salt and freshly cracked pepper	

1 In a large skillet, melt butter over a medium heat and add onion. Cook until golden, about 12 minutes. Add the sage and garlic and cook 2 or 3 minutes longer.
2 Transfer onion mixture to bowl and stir in the bread crumbs and egg.
3 Mix well and add cream while stirring. Season with salt and fresh cracked pepper and let cool before stuffing the bird.

Super-duper handy tip: One of the problems when stuffing a bird is that the outside (the delicious breast meat) cooks long before the inside does, as it takes longer for the heat to get in there and do its stuff. To ensure more even cooking, get yourself

a long-handled spoon (like one you would use to eat a tall ice cream sundae) and insert it handle first into the centre of the stuffed bird through the stuffing cavity. The spoon face and a bit of the handle should be left sticking out to act as a heat conductor to the middle of the bird.

Buffalo Eggplant Stew

1	large eggplant	1
3 1/2 lbs	buffalo stew meat	1.5 kg
3	medium onions, chopped	
1/3 cup	canola oil	75 ml
1 tsp	turmeric or curry powder	5 ml
1 tsp	salt	5 ml
1 1/4 quarts	water	1.25 L
1 cup	canned crushed tomatoes in their juices	250 ml
3 tbsp	tomato paste	45 ml
1 lb	assorted fresh mushrooms	450 g
	Juice of 1/2 lemon	
1/2 cup	freshly grated Parmesan cheese*	125 ml

There are several different grades of Parmesan cheese in the world. Parmesan Reggiano is widely considered the best, while the petroleum by-product that comes in a plastic shaker borders on inedible. For dishes like a casserole, we don't suggest using the Reggiano unless you've recently won the lottery. However, please consider using something other than the plastic shaker. Your taste buds will thank you.

Buffalo is a tasty, low-fat meat that requires about two-thirds of the cooking time of regular beef. Fat acts as an insulator (trust us on this one, we know from insulation) which heat must first penetrate before cooking the meat proteins. Buffalo has less fat, ergo less insulation, ergo less cooking time or a lower cooking temperature (for instance, a buffalo roast cooks at 275°F instead of the regular 325°F to 350°F). It also gets as tough as a boot camp drill sergeant if you overcook it, so be vedy vedy careful.

Serves 6 as a main course

1 Preheat oven to 350°F (180°C).
2 Cut eggplant into 1/3-inch (0.75-cm) slices and salt the slices to draw out the bitterness. Pat them dry after about an hour. Pan-fry in batches in a non-stick skillet until golden brown. Put aside to cool.
3 In a large Dutch oven, brown the buffalo meat and onion in the oil.
4 Add turmeric and salt and continue to brown for 2 minutes.
5 Add the water and bring to a boil. Cover and simmer until meat is cooked through, about 75 minutes.
6 Add tomatoes, tomato paste, mushrooms, and lemon juice and mix thoroughly.
7 Pour all the ingredients from the Dutch oven into a glass casserole and cover with slices of eggplant.
8 Bake in the oven for 45 minutes.
9 Sprinkle Parmesan cheese on top and continue to bake for about another 20 minutes.

Balsamico Traditionale

11

The "Balsamico Traditionale" episode took place on Vancouver Island, a little bit of heaven tucked up against mainland British Columbia. It rains a lot on Vancouver Island and it's warm and humid and lush and green and the pace is slower and the people get things done when they get things done and life is good and you can't get anywhere in a hurry because all roads wind along the coast. There we found a story of passion and unwavering commitment to excellence. A story about following your dreams and sharing with family. A story that made us proud to be Canadian.

Blink and you'll miss the unassuming entrance to the Venturi-Schulze winery off the Trans-Canada Highway on the east coast of Vancouver Island, smack dab in the middle of sunny Cowichan Valley. Giordano

and Marilyn, he of Venturi and she of Schulze, run this wonderful little vineyard with almost fanatical attention to producing a superior wine without pesticides or chemical assistance. The entire vineyard is covered in fine netting to keep out pesky birds and squirrels. Vines are planted farther apart than in larger commercial operations, allowing each and every grape to bask in the warm island sun. Venturi-Schulze wine is only available at select B.C. restaurants such as Sooke Harbour House and Diva at the Met, or through their newsletter (they refuse to ship during the warmer months!). The Venturi-Schulzes are a warm and generous family who consider their little piece of heaven to be more a way of life than a business. Generation #2 is now involved in the person of confident young daughter Michelle.

But terrific organic wines are not their only forte. Giordano hails from Spilamberto in Modena, Italy, and for the last 28 years he has been nurturing an incredible Aceto Balsamico vinegar, lovingly reduced over hand-stoked wood fires and then aged in barrels (imported from Modena) of chestnut, cherry, acacia, ash, and oak in the traditional manner that made his home province world famous. This is a syrupy, complex nectar the colour of smoked glass with a throbbing languid taste. Calling it vinegar somehow does not do it justice. It is as enjoyable by the snifter (accompanied by Parmesan shavings, of course!) as any wine.

Here's the best part: 1 cup (250 ml) of their Aceto Balsamico, a mixture of vinegar aged from 6 to 28 years, sells for a paltry $45, a fraction of the cost of a like product from Italy. If you're the plan ahead sort, 2004 will see the release of a vinegar begun at least 12 years before. What's the big deal? The rate of evaporation in creating this work of art will reduce some 1000 gallons of exquisite juice down to a scant 25 gallons! These people are true artists. Do yourself a favour and get your hands on their vinegar and wines.

Here are a number of recipes adapted from our travels on Vancouver Island and from the Venturi-Schulze kitchen.

Balsamic Rhubarb Compote

4	large stalks rhubarb	4
4 tbsp	balsamic vinegar	60 ml
1 1/4 cups	sugar	300 ml
1 tsp	peeled and grated fresh ginger	5 ml

1 Wash and dry the rhubarb stalks. Trim the ends and remove the leafy part. Cut the stalks into 1/2-inch (1-cm) pieces.
2 Combine the vinegar, sugar, and ginger in a medium saucepan over a medium heat and stir until the sugar has dissolved.
3 Add the rhubarb and mix well. Simmer without stirring for 3 minutes or until the rhubarb is semi-soft but still has a bit of a crunch to it, sort of al dente. Remove the rhubarb with tongs, shaking as much of the liquid as possible back into the saucepan. Transfer the rhubarb to a bowl.
4 Bring the liquid back to simmer and let it thicken for 5 to 7 minutes.
5 Remove the now syrupy liquid from the stove and stir in the rhubarb.
6 Serve immediately as a side to your pork dish.

Delicioso with a nice rosemary-crusted pork roast, with a pan-fried pork chop, or even as a final-minute glaze on a broiled pork tenderloin. This sweet and tart compote takes no time to make and will add a zing to your porco dish. Try it at room temperature on a leftover turkey sandwich. If you're not using "real" balsamic vinegar, taste the compote once or twice as it cooks in case you want to add an extra tablespoon of the commercial variety to up the balsamic taste, but watch that you don't burn your tongue! Substitute 3 cups (750 ml) of frozen chopped rhubarb when the fresh stuff is out of season.

Makes about 1 1/2 cups/375 ml

New Potato, Goat Cheese, and Green Bean Salad with Sweet Balsamic Vinaigrette

This is an excellent summer salad that goes perfectly with fried chicken or a cold fish entree. We suggest the world-famous French *haricots*, but any fresh thin green bean will do. If green beans are not available, try snow peas as a substitute. If goat cheese isn't your thing, replace it with the same amount of good-quality feta cheese.

Serves 6

For the dressing:

4 tbsp	balsamic vinegar	60 ml
3 tbsp	maple syrup	45 ml
2 tbsp	Dijon mustard	30 ml
1 tbsp	diced fresh rosemary	15 ml
1	garlic clove, finely diced	1
1/2 cup	olive oil	125 ml
	Salt and freshly cracked pepper	

For the salad:

1 1/2 lb	small new potatoes, skin on	675 g
3/4 lb	*haricots vert*, trimmed	350 g
1	small red onion, halved and thinly sliced	1
1/2	bunch fresh basil, washed and stems removed, torn into pieces	1/2
2	rolls of goat cheese (about 2/3 lb/300 g), kept in the fridge so it's hard enough to crumble	2

1 Mix all the dressing ingredients together and whisk until well blended. Adjust to your personal taste with more syrup, mustard, or vinegar. Set aside so that the flavours can blend.

2 Bring a large pot of water to a boil over high heat and add the potatoes. Boil them for 5 minutes or so, depending on their size, or until they're tender and cooked through. Using tongs or a slotted spoon, transfer the spuds to a large colander and then rinse well under cold water to halt the cooking process. Cut them into quarters or sixths, depending on their size, and set aside in a large serving bowl.

3 Add the *haricots vert* to the boiling water and cook for 4 or 5 minutes (this step is not necessary if you're using snow peas), until al dente. Drain them in the colander and rinse under cold water. Pat them dry with paper towel and snap them in half with your hands (allow them to break naturally when you bend them). Add them to the potatoes.

4 Add the red onion, basil, and dressing and toss well. Let sit for 5 minutes or so before serving.

5 Divide the salad among 6 serving plates and crumble the goat cheese over top.

Rosemary-Parmesan Mashed Potatoes

8–10	medium russet or Yukon Gold potatoes, peeled and cut into 1-inch/2.5-cm pieces	8–10
2 tbsp	unsalted butter	30 ml
2	sprigs fresh rosemary, coarsely chopped with stems discarded	2
1/2 cup	2% or homo milk	125 ml
	Salt and freshly cracked pepper	
1/2 cup	freshly grated Parmesan cheese	125 ml

1 Bring a large pot of salted water to boil over a high heat and add the potatoes. Boil until tender, about 7 minutes.

2 While the potatoes are boiling, melt the butter in a small skillet or saucepan over a medium-high heat and add the rosemary. Sauté for 3 or 4 minutes, allowing the essence of the rosemary to insinuate itself into the butter. Add the milk and reduce the heat to medium-low and continue cooking for another 3 minutes.

3 Once cooked, drain the potatoes in a colander and return them to the same pot. Pour in the rosemary liquid and mix well. Mash the potatoes (or use your hand blender, pulsing on and off until the spuds are smooth) until you get the consistency you like the best.

4 Season with salt and fresh cracked pepper and add the Parmesan cheese. Stir to mix well and cover. Let sit for 5 minutes before serving.

We like russets or Yukon Golds for our mashed potatofication purposes. However, if you go with a thinner-skinned spud, like a red or those little white ones, then leave the skins on the potatoes for an enhanced taste and texture. Also, we like the texture we get from using our hand mixer instead of mashing by hand. Others, however, prefer the manual mashing method (or *methode de mashing à la manual,* as it's known in your finer cooking schools), suggesting that the hand blender method offers a finished spud more closely approximating a purée than a mash.

Serves 6 as a side dish

Calf's Liver with Bacon, Herbs, and Balsamic Vinegar

Serves 6 as a main course

3 1/2 lbs	calf's liver	1.5 kg
	Salt and freshly cracked pepper	
1 lb	bacon slices, coarsely chopped	450 g
1/2 lb	unsalted butter	225 g
1	red onion, halved and thinly sliced	1
1	garlic clove, finely diced	1
3 tbsp	flour	45 ml
1/2 cup	balsamic vinegar	125 ml
1 1/2 cups	beef stock	375 ml
1 1/2 cups	chicken stock	375 ml
1 tbsp	dried sage	15 ml
1 tbsp	dried thyme	15 ml
1	bunch fresh chives (for garnish, optional)	1

1 Pat the calf's liver dry with paper towel and season with salt and fresh cracked pepper.

2 Fry the bacon in a large skillet over a medium heat until nice and crispy. Transfer the bacon to a bowl lined with paper towel and set aside.

3 Drain the bacon fat from the skillet and add the butter. Turn the heat up to medium-high and add the calf's liver once the butter has melted and begins to foam. Sauté, turning now and then, for about 4 minutes or until the pieces have firmed up when touched with tongs. Don't go much more than 5 minutes tops or the liver will dry out and taste like cafeteria food.

4 Remove the now-soggy paper towel from the bacon-filled bowl and return the bacon and the calf's liver to the bowl. Cover with tin foil to keep warm.

5 Pour off half the drippings from the pan and add the onion and garlic, which you'll sauté over a medium-high heat for 4 minutes or until the garlic turns golden brown. Sprinkle the flour around the skillet and then mix thoroughly. Continue to sauté for another 2 minutes.

6 Pour in the balsamic vinegar and bring to a boil. Scrape up all the juicy delicious brown bits that have been clinging to the bottom and sides of the skillet. Let the vinegar reduce for 2 minutes and add the two stocks and herbs. Let the liquid come back to a gentle

boil and reduce the heat to medium, and simmer for about 15 to 20 minutes until the liquid has reduced by at least half and has a thicker sauce-like consistency. Don't worry . . . trust your own judgement. Season to taste with salt and fresh cracked pepper.

7 Serve with Rosemary-Parmesan Mashed Potatoes (see recipe above) and Corn and Tomatoes in Basil-Balsamic Butter (recipe follows). Place a healthy mound of the potatoes in the middle of each serving plate. Mix the liver and bacon well and divide evenly among the plates, placing on top of the potatoes. Spoon the sauce over the liver and bacon, allowing it to run down into the potatoes, forming little pools of succulent nectar in which your tastes buds can swim and frolic. Spoon the corn and tomatoes around the potato mound. Lastly, embed 3 or 4 strands of chive in the mashed potatoes between pieces of the liver so that they stand up like a chive fireworks explosion of love and give additional height to the plate.

Corn and Tomatoes in Basil-Balsamic Butter

1/2 cup	unsalted butter	125 ml
2	shallots, finely diced	2
1 tbsp	balsamic vinegar	15 ml
6	ears of corn, shucked and kernels separated from the ears	6
4 tbsp	finely diced fresh basil	60 ml
18	cherry tomatoes, washed	18

Melt the butter in a medium saucepan over a medium-high heat and add the shallots and balsamic vinegar. Sauté for 2 minutes. Turn the heat down to medium and add the corn and fresh basil. Sauté for 4 minutes longer. Add the cherry tomatoes and sauté for another minute or so until the tomatoes have warmed through but before they get mooshy.

You can separate the (uncooked) corn kernels from the ear by standing the ear on its end (bad joke) and running a sharp knife along the ear from top to bottom in long strokes. If you can't find cherry tomatoes, use four quartered and seeded plum tomatoes instead.

Serves 6 as a side dish

Really Great Canadian Wheat

12

Canada grows the best wheat in the world. Period. *Point finale*. And while vast rolling prairie land of golden wheat that ripples in the wind is as much a Canadian icon as are Mounties and maple syrup, wheat is as new to this country as are the early immigrants.

Our wheat is the secret to the best breads in all the world, and bread is the foundation of modern civilization. It offers a pocked topography that so perfectly holds and melts butter into its crooks and nannies. And bread is *in*...whoa boy, is it in! After years, perhaps decades, of eating not-so-wonder bread, bleached white and devoid of any taste or nutrition, we're starting to eat all sorts of breads — dark breads, grain breads, sourdough breads, baguettes, buns, rolls, twists, bagels, focaccia, pitas, brioches, panattones, biscuits, blinis,

muffins, scones, squares, popovers, croissants, and crumpets. We're eating them all and life has never been better. In big cities and small towns, artisan bakers are setting up shop, perfuming the foggy haze with that incredible aroma that only fresh-baked delicacies can possibly give off. Perhaps, in time, as more and more of us take to the baking arts, great billows of this special aroma will escape through that hole in the ozone, wafting out into space and reaching a faraway world, thus proving that there is indeed intelligent and civilized life on the third planet from the sun.

As for the other great wheat treat — pasta — , well let's just say . . . ahhhh . . . the wonderful world of pasta. Spaghettini is just like spaghetti, only the noodles are thinner . . . but thicker still than vermicelli. Of course, then you've got your fettuccine and linguine, which are just like spaghetti and spaghettini . . . only flatter. And let's not even get started on fusilli, cappelletti, fettucce, lumache, pappardelle, penne, ziti, tagliatelle, quadrettini, creste di galli, and about a bazillion other pasta shapes, sizes, colours, flavours, stuffings, and cooking requirements. Whatever shape or size, pasta is best when made with Canadian semolina. Just ask the Italians; they're the biggest importers of Canadian semolina wheat in the world!

We went to the Prairies to do a story about the science of wheat and what has made it so universally popular (it's gluten, by the way), and we found these crazy wonderful scientists in lab coats who are gaga for what they do. These people live and breathe wheat (okay, so maybe they don't actually breathe wheat, but you get the general idea). It is a pleasure to find folk so committed to their work, so in love with what they do. In the original story line we were all supposed to end up at this cool pasta place called Deluca's for a big feed, but instead we ended up going back to one of the Wheat Board's employee's place to cook our brains out.

These are the recipes that Carlo came up with for this episode, each originating in his family's restaurant, and then there are some of our own. We have faithfully transposed them word for word from the original e-mail he sent us from his swingin' bachelor pad on College Street in Torontosaurus Rex.

Subject: A furrowed brow, a heroic presence, College Street. It was Pippa's tirade that finally brought me to my knees. I was lost, devastated. The inconceivable events of the previous week had thoroughly depleted me. My two stalwart friends from the seminary, the only two who could help, Derby and Faust, were unavailable. They had fled to Cap Ferrat after announcing their risky decision to become lovers. I looked solemnly down from my mansard apartments at the throng below . . . Yikes, I am terribly, unequivocally sorry. The fact of the matter is that writing has just broken out on College Street and we must squash it, sir, like a bug.

Here are a couple of recipes for ya.

MAINTAIN TOP SAFE SPEED

Gnocchi alla Gorgonzola

1 Put ½ cup (125 ml) of heavy cream in a skillet over medium heat.
2 Add a honkin' great slab of gorgonzola and let the cheese meet the cream.
3 Briefly cook ½ lb/225 g of gnocchi in salted boiling water, then throw 'em in with the reduced gorgo-cream magic. Add parmesan cheese if you like.

If you are over the age of 26, have yourself driven immediately to a location that has CPR facilities. Heart attacks after eating this dish are very common.

This recipe is delightfully simple.

Serves 2 as a main course

Homemade Ravioli Stuffed with Roasted Squash and Goat Cheese in Frangelico Butter Sauce

This recipe is considerably more simple than it sounds. We have made this as an appetizer on numerous occasions to rave reviews. The walnut taste of the Frangelico sets off the creaminess of the goat cheese coupled with the nuttiness of the roasted squash. You can double the quantity and serve this dish as a main course. You'll be serving everybody three large ravioli, which you'll make yourself from fresh sheets of lasagna pasta you can buy at an Italian deli or fine food store. Make this recipe once and it's like sleepwalking every time after that. It looks difficult but it's all a delicious illusion. Go for it! You have nothing to fear but pasta itself.

Serves 6 as an appetizer

For the ravioli:

	Olive oil	
3 1/2 lbs	butternut squash, halved and seeded	1.5 kg
2 tbsp	unsalted butter	30 ml
6	shallots, finely diced	6
2	garlic cloves, finely diced	2
1 tsp	dried sage	5 ml
1 tsp	dried savory	5 ml
3 1/2 oz	goat cheese, at room temperature	100 g
	Salt and freshly cracked pepper	
12	sheets fresh lasagna pasta (multi-coloured is cool)	12

For the sauce:

1/2 cup	unsalted butter	125 ml
1/2 cup	hazelnuts, toasted and skinned, coarsely chopped	125 ml
4 tbsp	Frangelico liqueur	60 ml

1 Preheat oven to 400°F (200°C). Pour a little olive oil on your hands and rub the exposed face of each squash half. Place the squash cut-side-down on a baking sheet and cook in the middle of the oven for about 40 minutes or until the flesh turns a deep orangey-brown. Remove the squash from the oven and let it cool for a bit. Scoop the flesh into a large mixing bowl and chuck the skin.

2 Meanwhile, melt the butter in a medium saucepan over medium-high heat and add the shallots. Cook for 4 minutes and lower the heat to medium. Add the garlic, sage, and savory and cook for 2 minutes, being sure not to burn the garlic. Add the shallot mixture to the squash and stir to mix well. Add the goat cheese and mix until all the ingredients are bound together and you have a gooey, cheesy garlic-squash filling. Season to taste with salt and freshly cracked pepper.

3 Bring a large pot of salted water to a gentle boil. Divide the pasta sheets into 2 stacks of 6 sheets each. Using a very sharp knife, cut

the sheets into thirds. Don't worry if they're not perfect squares. Cover the stack with a damp towel so they won't dry out.

4   Get a small glass of water and a pastry brush. Take 2 of the pasta squares from the pile and cover the rest with the wet towel again. Place 1 of the squares on your work surface and brush its edges with water. Mound a spoonful of the filling on the middle of the square and flatten it out just a wee bit with the back of a spoon. There should be a good ¼-inch (0.5 cm) or so left around the edges. Place the second pasta square on top and press down along the edges, working out any air pockets or lumps. Brush the edges of the top square with a bit more water and score the edges using the tines of a fork. Repeat the process with the remaining pasta squares.

5   Cook the ravioli 4 or 5 at a time in a pot of gently boiling water. The key word here is "gently." Cook for 5 or 6 minutes, or until the ravioli float to the top and seem pliable. Remove the ravioli with a slotted spoon and transfer them to a casserole dish. Add about 1 cup (250 ml) of the boiling water to the casserole dish and cover with plastic wrap. Repeat the cooking process with the remaining ravioli.

6   While your last batch is bubbling away, prepare the sauce. Melt the butter in a small saucepan. Add the hazelnuts and Frangelico and simmer for 4 minutes. Do not bring to a boil or the butter will burn!

7   Transfer the ravioli from the water bath with a slotted spoon, making sure that the excess water drips off the ravioli first. Plate 3 ravioli per serving. If you were lucky enough to get multi-coloured pasta, place 1 of each colour on each plate. Drizzle the hazelnut butter over the ravioli and spoon the nuts from the sauce around the plates. Serve immediately.

Tagliatelle al Pollo

This is also known as the Do or Die or the Black Monday Tagliatelle because of the armed insurrection we faced in the restaurant when we attempted to take it off the menu. There is nothing more vicious than a north Toronto Protestant housewife. A word about the choice of pasta: You can use any type of noodle to make this dish, but the long flat (or ruffled edge) tagliatelle offers the best support for the sauce. A thinner or shorter noodle would find it hard to compete with the reduced cream, tomato, and delicious slices of chicken. The best tomato sauce to use is the kind that you make at home and keep knocking around in the fridge. Open two or three tins of good plum tomatoes and pass them through a sieve, chop 'em up, or throw 'em in a pot and mash 'em with a sturdy whisk. Let 'em melt over low heat until they reach a rich saucy texture.

Serves 4

2	chicken breasts, cut into strips	2
	Flour (for dredging)	
2 tbsp	olive oil	30 ml
1	medium onion, very finely chopped	1
1 cup	white wine	250 ml
4 cups	tomato sauce	1 L
1/2 cup	heavy cream	125 ml
1 lb	tagliatelle pasta	450 g

1 Dredge the chicken strips in flour and toss them into a skillet with very hot olive oil.
2 As the chicken starts to brown, throw in the onion.
3 As the onions turn translucent and start to brown, the chicken will continue to brown. Drain off excess oil, stand back, and add the white wine.
4 Let the pan deglaze and add the tomato sauce.
5 As the tomato sauce reduces, add the cream.
6 In a pot of boiling water, cook tagliatelle until al dente. Fish 'em out and toss with sauce. Eat, drink, love.

Penne with Sausages and Sun-Dried Tomatoes

2 tbsp	olive oil	30 mL
1	medium onion, finely chopped	1
1 tsp	dried rosemary	5 ml
2–3 pinches	chili flakes	2–3 pinches
3	garlic cloves	3
4	your favourite sausages, sliced into bite-size pieces	4
1/2 cup	sun-dried tomatoes, thinly sliced	125 ml
4 cups	tomato sauce	1 L
1 lb	penne	450 g

1 Heat olive oil in a skillet and toss in the onions, a little rosemary and two or three pinches of chili flakes.
2 Using a garlic press, squeeze in the garlic.
3 Throw in the sausages and let them sizzle until slightly crisp.
4 Add the sun-dried tomatoes.
5 By this point the onions will be beginning to brown. Add the tomato sauce.
6 Allow everything to reduce while you browse through your favourite magazine.
7 Add penne to a pot of boiling water and cook until al dente.
8 Toss with sauce and serve, laugh, and conceive.

This dish is a must for the long winter nights. The sausage distressingly has been linked (get it?) to naughty mystery meat. Indeed, companies of ill repute have been churning out bangers that we wouldn't feed to the raccoons on our roof. But I say this: It is time for men to readdress the sausage. After all, did not a sausage journey with Magellan? Wasn't Columbus' mom stuffing 'em for her son the night he said, "Shall I bring you back a scarf, Mommy?" When our boys braved the capricious tides at Dieppe in their holy struggle against the Hun, what were they noshing? That's right, dear chappie, the standard-issue fennel and sage sausage.

Serves 4

Linguine with Clams, Tomatoes, and Arugula

This is an unbelievably easy recipe with big taste payback. As always, a recipe this simple requires the freshest and best ingredients possible. If you absolutely cannot find fresh clams, go with the canned variety but remember: Whether fresh or canned, get the little guys. When it comes to clams, the bigger they are, the chewier they are. Ideally you want 6 to 12 clams per person, depending on the size of the clams (you'd want 12 Manilas or 6 or so Littlenecks), so use your best judgement. This recipe features arugula (which sounds like a university drinking cry, as in AH-ROOOOO-GOO-LAH). We've got a big whopper bunch o' garlic in here, which you can adjust according to your tastes, but we would suggest at least one clove per serving. If you are so inclined, you can also substitute shrimp for the clams.

Serves 6 as a main course, unless you're a traditional Italian, in which case this dish comes about halfway through the main courses

1 1/2 lbs	linguine for six people	675 g
4 tbsp	olive oil	60 ml
6	shallots, finely diced	6
10	garlic cloves, finely diced	10
36–75	fresh clams (depending on their size)	36–75
4	plum tomatoes, peeled and seeded, then coarsely chopped	4
1/2–1 cup	dry white wine (depending on how many clams are used)	125–250 ml
1 1/2 lbs	fresh arugula, washed and roughly torn, stems removed	675 ml

1 Cook the linguine as per directions on the package or from the pasta maker until al dente. You don't want to cook the pasta all the way, as you're going to finish it off in the saucepan.
2 Heat the olive oil in a large saucepan over a medium heat and add the shallots and garlic. Sauté them for 2 or 3 minutes or until the shallots are translucent . . . watch that you don't burn the garlic.
3 Add the clams and tomatoes. Stir and add the wine. Cover the pot and cook for 7 or 8 minutes or until the clams have opened. Remove the clams from the saucepan to a warming bowl with tongs or a big slotted spoon. Discard any of the clams that have not opened.
4 Add the pasta and arugula to the saucepan and toss well.
5 Divide the pasta among the serving plates and top with the clams. Serve with a fruity white wine or a blonde beer, crusty bread, and marinated olives.

Penne with Mushrooms and Proscuitto

1 lb	penne	450 g
2 cups	chicken stock	500 ml
1 1/2 cups	35% cream	375 ml
2 tbsp	unsalted butter	30 ml
1/2 tsp	crushed dried hot pepper flakes	2 ml
2	garlic cloves, finely diced	2
6	large portobello mushroom caps, halved and sliced about 1/4 inch/0.5 cm thick	6
2 cups	baby green peas, fresh or thawed if using frozen	500 ml
12	slices proscuitto, sliced thinly against the grain	12
1 cup	grated Parmesan cheese	250 ml
	Salt and freshly cracked pepper	

1 Cook the penne until almost done, al dente as they say in fancy restaurants, and set aside.

2 Bring the stock and cream to a boil in a large pot over a medium-high heat. Reduce the heat to medium and allow the liquid to bubble away for about 30 minutes or until thickened and reduced by half.

3 Meanwhile, melt the butter in a medium saucepan over a medium heat and add the hot pepper flakes, garlic, and mushrooms. Sauté until the mushrooms have browned and most of the liquid they give off has evaporated.

4 Add the drained pasta and mushroom mixture to the cream sauce and mix well. Add the peas, proscuitto, and Parmesan cheese and season with salt and fresh cracked pepper. Stir again until well blended and cover tightly. Let stand for 3 minutes so the flavours can blend.

5 Divide the pasta onto 6 serving plates and top with additional Parmesan cheese.

The great thing about pasta recipes is that so many of the ingredients can be changed. Instead of mushrooms you can use a pork tenderloin (yes, a pork tenderloin cut into medallion-sized slices). Instead of proscuitto you can use any other cured ham (like pancetta), or even bacon in a pinch. Go for the proscuitto though as it has a salty taste that is nicely offset by the cream and garlic. Of course, any other tubular or small-sized pasta can be substituted for the penne.

This is a rich, mouth-watering recipe that is quite easy to make. Enjoy.

Serves 6

Lunenburg Lobster 13

Okay, we love the Maritimes. We love the hospitality, we love the people, we love the rum. As landlubbers "from away," however, we're a little confused as to who is and who isn't a Maritimer. As we understand it, Nova Scotia, Prince Edward Island, and New Brunswick are Maritime provinces. Newfoundland isn't, although it sits out there in the middle of the ocean. Newfoundland IS however, an Atlantic Canada province (as are the three Maritime provinces). Quebec isn't, although it too borders on the Atlantic Ocean. And as for British Columbia, well it is neither a Maritime province nor a Pacific province, even though it probably has more oceanfront coastline than all of the Atlantic provinces combined! Very confusing.

Titular confusion not withstanding, each of them provinces out there in the Atlantic is a wonderful place

filled with warm, friendly folk, an easy cadence to life, and lots of great food. Lunenburg, Nova Scotia, is as pretty a working fishing port as you're going to find anywhere in the world. It is also home to big, juicy, butter-drenched lobsters.

Steamed or boiled, lobster is meant to be consumed with orgasmic enthusiasm. A properly consumed lobster will leave you with juices running down your chin, a pile of cracked shells on your plate, and a very satisfied grin on your face. The locals pride themselves on knowing how to get every last bit of lobster meat out of those shells without so much as a fork, let alone a nutcracker. We should use every modern invention at our disposal to dig out those hidden nuggets…and for God's sake, whatever you do don't throw out the tomale or the roe! They're both yummy when spread on crusty bread with a splash of lemon juice.

However, we do recognize that some folk might be intimidated by the thought of tackling a whole steaming lobster. Here then are recipes inspired by our many visits out east that serve up the venerable lobster in a few different ways.

Roasted Lobster with Lemon Chive Oil

1 cup	olive oil	250 ml
2	bunches fresh chives	2
	Salt and white pepper, to taste	
6	live lobsters	6
2	lemons	2

In this recipe you only boil the lobsters long enough to send them to that big lobster trap in the sky, then finish them off in the oven. The lemon chive oil is a delicious change from the standard drawn butter.

Serves 6 as a main course

1 Preheat your oven to 400°F (200°C).
2 In a blender or food processor, purée the olive oil and chives. Add salt and white pepper to taste. Set aside.
3 Bring a very large pot of water to boil over a high heat. Plunge 2 of the lobsters into the boiling water headfirst. Don't do more than 2 at a time or it will take too long to return the water to a boil and the lobsters won't cook properly. Boil them for 3 minutes only. Remove and repeat with the remaining lobsters.
4 Place the lobsters belly-up on a cutting board. Using a large sharp knife, cut the lobsters in half lengthwise. Put an oven mitt on the hand holding the lobster for this step so as not to burn yourself on the hot lobster shells.
5 Place the lobsters cut-side-up on baking sheets and brush with two-thirds of the chive oil.
6 Roast lobsters in the oven for 25 minutes.
7 Remove them from the oven and brush with remaining chive oil. Squeeze lemons over the lobsters.
8 On each plate, place two lobster halves on a bed of mixed greens. Serve with warm crusty bread, unsalted butter, and lots of white wine.

The Fabled Maritime Lobster Roll

To an Upper Canada landlubber, there is something downright perverse about the Maritime lobster roll. We of big cities and freshwater lakes tend to consider lobster to be a delicacy to be consumed on special occasions, or when someone else is buying. The idea of that juicy one-of-a-kind lobster meat served up with mayo on a hot dog bun of all things is akin to painting a moustache on the *Mona Lisa* or laying down a dance track under a Mozart sonata or painting a poodle's toenails red. Okay, maybe not the poodle thing, but all the other stuff for sure! Nevertheless, wherever our travels took us along the east coast, there it was in restaurants and roadhouses, in truck stops and roadside diners. Even the Golden Starches had a McLobster McRoll.

So here then is the traditional lobster roll, although we understand there is a multitude of regional variations on the theme. Actually, it's a great way to stretch that expensive lobster by using all those great bits of meat from the knuckles, legs, and carapace. Might we suggest you consider a sourdough bun or baguette or pita pocket as a substitute for the hot dog bun? A dash of Tabasco sauce or some freshly diced cilantro would give your roll a nice zing as well. We've also substituted guacamole for mayonnaise and crab for lobster with great results.

Serves 6 for lunch

3 cups	diced lobster meat, already cooked	750 ml
6 tbsp	mayonnaise	90 ml
1	celery stalk, diced	1
	Juice of 1/2 lemon	
	Salt and freshly cracked pepper	
6	hot dog buns, toasted and buttered	6

1 Combine the lobster meat, mayonnaise, celery, and lemon juice in a bowl. Season with salt and fresh cracked pepper.
2 Pile the lobster mixture into the hot dog buns and serve with potato salad and buttermilk slaw (see Chapter 21 for recipe).

Telderberry Wines

14

In deciding what stories make it into the series, we have been quite aware of the danger of becoming a "restaurant show," travelling the country going from restaurant to restaurant, asking the same questions over and over again. Boring. Mind candy. TV filler. No thanks.

Bob Telder is a wonderful, bigger-than-life character who runs a berry farm about 45 minutes outside of Halifax, Nova Scotia. He loves his berries and has tremendous pride in the produce he delivers to market. The thing about berry wine (particularly blueberry wine) is that it can easily taste like very bad red grape wine (the kind that comes in a bag). But not Bob's, no siree. Bob's wine has complexity, it has a bit of carbonation to tickle your throat, and it tastes great!

But at some point we had to actually cook something! So we went to Dale Nichols, executive chef at the Chateau Halifax, and asked him to meet us at Bob's place. Dale packed up his pots and pans and drove out to the farm, where he cooked us a wonderful multi-course feast using Bob's amazing berry wines. It turned out to be an exceptional story because Dale "made do" with Bob's non-professional, non-restaurant kitchen. In other words, he dazzled us in the same sort of kitchen that we all have at home, proving that you don't have to have state-of-the-art equipment and a brigade of sous-chefs to do killer cuisine. This story resonated with our

viewers and garnered a tremendous amount of mail. It served as a reminder for us to cook outside of big industrial kitchens.

The first two recipes call for poaching, which is simply the technique of gently cooking food in a liquid just below the boiling point. This process infuses the poached ingredient with the essence and flavour of the poaching liquid.

Baby Spinach and Mushroom Salad with Gorgonzola Cheese and Pears Poached in Strawberry Wine with Orange Vinaigrette

Gorgonzola is what we used to call "stinky-sock cheese" as kids. Named for the small Italian town from whence it came, gorgonzola is a rich and pungent blue-streaked cow's milk cheese. Even if you don't normally go for strong cheeses, give this recipe a try, as the cheese is perfectly offset by the sweetness of the pears and the acidity of the vinaigrette. The Anjou pear is firm and sweet with a delicate greenish-yellow skin highlighted with a red blush. No Anjous? Substitute another pear, but consult with your grocer to make sure it's a sweet one.

If strawberry wine is not in your pantry, try puréeing some strawberries and then strain them through a very fine sieve while pushing down on the solids with the back of a wooden spoon. Add the resulting juice to a nice light white wine a couple of teaspoonfuls at a time until you've reached a taste you like.

Serves 6 as a starter

For the orange vinaigrette:

	Juice of 2 large, ripe oranges	
	(Valencia would be really nice)	
1/2 tsp	finely grated orange rind	2 ml
2 tbsp	balsamic vinegar	30 ml
2 tbsp	white wine vinegar	30 ml
1	shallot, finely diced	1
	Salt and freshly cracked pepper, to taste	
3/4 cup	unsaturated oil of your choice	175 ml
1 1/2 tbsp	chopped fresh tarragon leaves	20 ml
	(or 1/2 tsp/2 ml dried)	

1 In a small saucepan, bring the orange juice and rind to a boil over medium-high heat. Reduce heat to medium and simmer for a couple of minutes, until the liquid has reduced by three-quarters, thus intensifying the orange flavour.
2 In a bowl, combine the orange reduction with the vinegars, shallot, salt, and freshly cracked pepper. Mix well.
3 Add the oil by pouring in a stream while whisking. Add the tarragon and whisk for a few seconds longer. Adjust taste with salt and freshly cracked pepper.

For the salad:

3	Anjou pears, cored, halved, and peeled	3
3	bunches fresh baby spinach, washed and with hard stems removed	3
1/2 lb	assorted mushrooms, cleaned* and thinly sliced	225 g
3/4 lb	gorgonzola cheese, cut into bite-size cubes	340 g

* *See Chapter 8 for the what's what on cleaning mushrooms.*

For the poaching liquid:

1	bottle (3 cups/750 ml) Telderberry strawberry wine	1
1 cup	water	250 ml
4 tbsp	brown sugar	60 ml
2	cinnamon sticks	2
1/2 tsp	ground nutmeg	1 ml

1 Combine all ingredients for the poaching liquid in a pan large enough to hold all of the pears in one layer. Bring to a rapid boil over a high heat. Reduce heat to medium-low and simmer for 30 minutes.

2 Add pears to the poaching liquid in one layer. Cover with tin foil, pressing down to submerge the pears as much as possible. Simmer until the pears are soft to the touch of a fork.

3 Remove pears to cool and discard the poaching liquid. Slice each pear half into 8 slices.

4 Toss spinach with the orange vinaigrette and divide among 6 serving plates.

5 Top the spinach with mushrooms and gorgonzola cheese. Fan pear slices on top and serve.

Maritime Oyster Chowder with Telderberry Apple Wine and Sweet Curried Whipped Cream

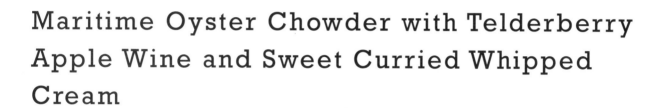

3 tbsp	unsalted butter	45 ml
1	medium onion, cut into strips à la julienne	1
24	Malpeque oysters, shucked with juice reserved	24
1 tbsp	chopped garlic	15 ml
3 tbsp	flour	45 ml
1 cup	Telderberry apple wine	250 ml
1 1/2 quarts	fish stock	1.5 L
1	large Granny Smith apple, cored and diced	1
2	medium potatoes, peeled and diced into small cubes	2
1/4 lb	red and yellow peppers, diced	115 g
1/2	bunch parsley, chopped	1/2
1/2 cup	35% cream	125 ml
	Salt and freshly cracked pepper	

This recipe calls for the mighty Malpeque oyster, possibly the tastiest bivalve in the world (see Chapter 20 for the skinny on oysters). Fear not if there ain't no Malpeques available, as any oyster will do as long as it is fresh. Shucking an oyster is not as daunting a task as it first might appear. It can be a bit messy, however. If you get your fishmonger to shuck 'em for you, make sure you get the oyster liquid as well.

If you can't get your hands on apple wine, substitute a regular white wine flavoured to taste with apple juice or apple cider. You can try apple cider in a pinch, but cut it with some water, as it naturally has a stronger apple taste than apple wine.

Serves 6 as a starter

1 In a large soup pot, melt the butter over a medium heat. Add the onion, oysters, and garlic and cook for 4 minutes.

2 Add the flour and stir gently until incorporated into the butter. Cook for 1 minute longer.

3 Add the apple wine a bit at a time, stirring all the while to avoid any lumps forming.

4 Add the stock and oyster juice and bring the liquid to a boil over a medium-high heat.

5 Add the apple and potato dice. Reduce heat to medium and simmer until potato is tender, about 5 minutes.

6 Add the sweet peppers, parsley, and cream. Season to taste with salt and freshly cracked pepper.

7 Spoon Sweet Curried Whipped Cream (recipe follows) on top of each bowl of soup just before serving.

Sweet Curried Whipped Cream

1 tbsp	unsalted butter	15 ml
1	small onion, finely diced	1
1/2	Granny Smith apple, cored, peeled, and diced	1/2
1/2	banana, cut into chunks	1/2
2 tbsp	curry powder	30 ml
Pinch	salt	Pinch
1/2 cup	35% cream	125 ml

1 In a small saucepan, melt the butter over a medium heat and add the onion. Sauté for 3 minutes.

2 Add the apple, banana, and curry powder. Stir well and roughly mash the ingredients together for 2 minutes longer. Add salt and stir again.

3 Purée in a food processor or blender. Set aside to cool.

4 In a large bowl, whip the cream until stiff peaks begin to form. Fold in the fruit mixture and mix well.

5 Spoon on top of the hot soup just before serving.

Filet of Atlantic Halibut Poached in Telderberry Pear Wine with Pear Wine Butter Sauce

6	Atlantic halibut filets	6
	(about 1/4 lb/115 g each, skin on)	
	Salt and freshly cracked pepper	

For the poaching liquid:

1	medium onion, chopped	1
1 tsp	coarsely chopped garlic	5 ml
2	bay leaves	2
2 cups	fish stock	500 ml
2 cups	Telderberry pear wine	500 ml
	Juice of 1 lemon	
1/2 tsp	fresh cracked pepper	2 ml

1 In a large skillet, combine the ingredients for the poaching liquid and bring to a boil over a medium-high heat. Reduce heat to medium-low and simmer for 30 minutes.

2 Add the halibut and cook for about 8 minutes, checking for desired doneness.

3 Remove the halibut and season with salt and fresh cracked pepper. Serve with Pear Wine Butter Sauce (recipe follows).

Pear Wine Butter Sauce

1/2 cup + 1 tbsp	unsalted butter, chilled and cut into cubes	125 g + 15 ml
1	shallot, finely chopped	1
1 cup	Telderberry pear wine	250 ml
1 cup	fish stock	250 ml
	Juice of 1 lemon	
1 tbsp	35% cream	15 ml
1	pear, cored, peeled, and diced	1
2 tbsp	coarsely chopped fresh parsley	30 ml
	Salt and fresh cracked pepper to taste	

1 In a small saucepan, melt 1 tbsp (15 ml) of unsalted butter over a medium-high heat and sauté the shallots for 1 minute.

2 Add the pear wine, fish stock, and lemon juice and bring to a gentle boil. Reduce heat to medium and simmer until the liquid has reduced by three-quarters.

Like all good chefs, Dale Nichols is always on the lookout for the freshest local ingredients available, ergo this recipe calls for Atlantic halibut. Pacific will do just nicely as well, although it is a bit less fatty than its Atlantic cousin (same-same for the salmon, same-same for the oysters). Either way, the best halibut is, of course, Canadian. Halibut can grow to the size of a small car and have been reported as weighing in at over 1000 pounds (500 kilograms). The ones we eat are of the smaller variety, caught while still young and tender. The meat is low-fat, tender, and mild in flavour, making it perfect for poaching.

If you can't get your hands on pear wine, then try puréeing a canned pear, then strain it through a fine sieve while pushing down on the solids with the back of a wooden spoon. Add the resulting liquid to white wine a few teaspoonfuls at a time until you reach a desired taste. If that's not in the cards, this recipe works just as well by simply using white wine.

Serves 6

3 Reduce heat to low. Add the cream and whisk in the remaining butter 1 piece at a time until a sauce consistency is achieved.

4 Add pear dice and parsley. Season to taste with salt and fresh cracked pepper.

Pan-Fried Medallions of Veal Striploin with Telderberry Blueberry Wine Reduction and Sage Oil

Veal striploin is readily available at any decent butcher store. This is an amazingly easy recipe that you would expect from a top-drawer restaurant. If you can't get a hold of blueberry wine, substitute a light fruity red – ask the wine specialist at your liquor store for advice. If your liquor store doesn't have a wine consultant, then take your business elsewhere . . . you deserve better.

Serves 6 as a main course

12	veal striploin medallions (about 3 oz/85 g each)	12
4 tbsp	canola oil	60 ml
2 tbsp	finely chopped fresh rosemary	30 ml
2 tbsp	finely chopped fresh thyme	30 ml
	Salt and fresh cracked pepper to taste	

1 Pat the veal medallions dry with paper towel.

2 Rub the veal with some of the canola oil and sprinkle with the rosemary and thyme. Season with salt and fresh cracked pepper.

3 In a large skillet, heat the remaining oil over a medium-high heat until very hot and almost smoking.

4 In 2 batches, sear the veal medallions for 90 seconds per side. Remove the veal to a warming plate and tent with tin foil to keep warm. Do not wash the skillet, as you are about to use it to make the sauce!

5 Serve the veal medallions drizzled with the blueberry sauce and sage oil (recipes follow) and with roasted or mashed potatoes and fresh seasonal veggies.

Blueberry Sauce

1	shallot, finely diced	1
1/2 tsp	finely diced garlic	2 ml
1/2 tsp	finely chopped fresh rosemary	2 ml
1/2 tsp	finely chopped fresh thyme	2 ml
1 cup	Telderberry blueberry wine	250 ml
2 cups	chicken stock	500 ml
1/2 pint	fresh wild blueberries	250 ml
1/3 cup	cold unsalted butter	80 ml
	Salt and fresh cracked pepper to taste	

1 In the pan you used to sear the veal medallions, sauté the shallot, garlic, and fresh herbs over medium heat for 1 minute.
2 Deglaze the pan with the blueberry wine, scraping the bottom and sides of the pan to release the succulent brown tidbits. Reduce the wine by half and add the chicken stock. Bring the liquids to a boil over medium-high heat. Reduce the heat to medium-low and simmer until a sauce consistency has been achieved, roughly 8 to 10 minutes.
3 Add the blueberries and whisk in the butter. Season to taste with salt and fresh cracked pepper.

Sage Oil

1	bunch fresh parsley, stems removed	1
1/2 cup	coarsely chopped fresh sage leaves	125 ml
1 cup	canola oil	250 ml
	Salt and fresh cracked pepper	

1 Blanch the parsley in a pot of boiling water for 5 seconds.
2 Transfer the parsley to a bowl full of ice water to stop the cooking process immediately and to retain the brilliant green colour.
3 Drain, dry, and roughly chop the parsley.
4 Place the blanched parsley, sage, and canola oil in a blender or food processor. Pulse the blender a few times until the ingredients are well mixed, then run the blender on high for 15 seconds.
5 Strain through a fine sieve and season to taste with salt and fresh cracked pepper.

Serve the veal medallions drizzled with the blueberry sauce and sage oil, roasted or mashed potatoes, and fresh seasonal veggies.

15

Les Chefs des Chefs and the Beaver Club

"Tell me what you eat and I will tell you what you are."
Jean Anthelme Brillat-Savarin

We found out about this story on a scant 24-hours' notice. After six months of planning and carefully selecting stories, all of sudden we get a run-of-the-mill, oh-by-the-way press release about *Les Chefs des Chefs* convening in Montreal . . . with Paul Bocuse in attendance . . . at the Beaver Club, no less! *Les Chefs des Chefs* is an exclusive little club made up of those chefs who cook for world leaders, royalty, and potentates. Paul Bocuse is generally considered one of the greatest living chefs, and the Beaver Club is possibly Canada's most venerable dining facility, with a history that goes back hundreds of years. Induction into the Beaver Club involves smok-

ing a peace pipe, drinking a secret brew called "loogaroo," and kissing a live black bear . . . and you thought the Freemasons were tough to get into. There were many harried last-minute negotiations because of all the governments involved, but we prevailed and quickly assembled our crew, jumping into a van and making our way to the Queen Elizabeth Hotel in downtown Montreal, home to the Beaver Club.

We found an august assembly of international uber-chefs good-naturedly taking part in this most Canadian of induction ceremonies. Meanwhile, Executive Chef Jean Cordeau and his brigade were going nuts in the kitchen, making dinner for a guest list used to having the best of the best on hand in their own kitchens. We shot the whole thing in about eight hours (most stories take two or three days to shoot), and the resulting story bounced back and forth between the tension in the kitchen and the fun in the club. The bear-kissing was left out of the final cut, as some people felt it was not politically correct to show such a magnificent animal performing for the assembly.

Here then are some of the recipes from that very special evening.

Smoked Salmon and Arctic Char Tartare with Herb Sauce

For the tartare:

2/3 lb	smoked salmon, sliced	300 g
3/4 lb	Arctic char, finely diced	350 g
3 tbsp	capers, drained and coarsely chopped	45 ml
	Juice of 1 lemon	
3	shallots, minced	3

Combine all ingredients in a bowl and mix well. Refrigerate for at least 1 hour to allow flavours to blend.

For the herb sauce:

1 1/4 cups	sour cream	300 ml
3 tbsp	finely chopped fresh herbs*	45 ml
1 tbsp	white wine	15 ml
	Salt and fresh cracked pepper to taste	

* *Use whatever herbs are in season or in your garden, such as sage, parsley, chives, thyme, or rosemary.*

Combine all ingredients in a bowl and refrigerate for at least 1 hour so that the flavours can blend.

To serve:

1 Preheat your oven to 350°F (180°C). Cut 6 slices from a baguette or French loaf, each slice about 1 inch (2.5 cm) thick. Toast the bread slices in the oven until golden brown. Remove from oven and let cool.

2 Cut a garlic clove in half. Rub the flat side of 1 of the clove halves over the toasted bread slices.

3 Mound one-sixth of the tartare on 1 of the toasted bread slices.

4 Cover the face of a small serving plate with one-sixth of the herb sauce and place the bread slice on top. Repeat with the other 5 slices and serve.

5 You may want to make extra toasted baguette slices for the middle of the table.

Beware unscrupulous retailers who will try to pass off inferior warm-water char as Arctic char. The real McCoy has a darker meat and a considerably more flavourful taste. As with all recipes requiring so few ingredients and so little preparation, the better the ingredients, the better the finished plate... As always, keep raw ingredients in the fridge until the last possible moment.

Serves 6 as a starter

Roast Loin of Caribou Lac St. Jean with Smoked Corn and Buckwheat Croquette and Berry Chutney in Blueberry Poivrade

Not surprisingly, the venerable *Larousse Gastronomique* (1990 edition) makes no mention whatsoever of caribou, as it is strictly a "colonial" delicacy.

All caribou is venison, but not all venison is caribou. Which is to say that "venison" is a catch-all term that refers to such diverse offerings as elk, deer, moose, and, of course, caribou. Farm-raised venison will be less gamy than its wild counterpart. You take your chances when you buy wild game, as you are never sure of its origins and how it was killed. As with sushi-grade tuna, unless the animal's death is unexpected and instantaneous, massive amounts of adrenalin will be released into the bloodstream, rendering the meat tough and chewy.

Try caribou if you can. It is the only "wild" game meat still available on the market. Everything else is farm-raised by law and the caribou is slaughtered annually by native bands in northern Quebec. If you can't find caribou, substitute a nice beef tenderloin steak, at least an inch (2.5 cm) thick.

This recipe calls for fresh Quebec blueberries, as Chef Cordeau insists on the best local ingredients possible. You can use any fresh blueberries you want. Blueberry vinegar is readily available at most supermarkets at a very reasonable price.

Serves 6

For the croquette:

Buckwheat flour is readily available at bulk food or health food stores. If you can't find smoked corn, then the same quantity of well-drained canned corn will do just as well.

1 1/2 cups	buckwheat flour	375 ml
3/4 tsp	baking powder	3 ml
3/4 lb	smoked corn niblets	340 g
1	egg, beaten	1
2 cups	milk (not skim milk, please)	500 ml
2 tbsp	unsalted butter	30 ml

1 Preheat your oven to 350°F (180°C).
2 Mix the buckwheat flour, baking powder, and corn together in a large bowl.
3 Whip in the egg and milk until a batter consistency is achieved (like a big pancake).
4 Melt the butter in a medium cast-iron skillet over a medium heat. Pour in the batter and swirl the pan to even it out. Do not stir once it's in the pan.
5 Cook for 3 minutes and finish in the oven until bubbly and golden brown.
6 Remove from the oven and cool on a plate or baking rack. Cut into 6 triangular pieces.

For the caribou:

2 tbsp	canola oil	30 ml
6	caribou loin steaks	6
	(just under 1/2 lb/225 g each)	
	Salt and fresh cracked pepper to taste	
1/3 cup	blueberry vinegar	75 ml
4 tbsp	crabapple, red currant, or cranberry jam	60 ml
1 pint	fresh blueberries	500 ml
1/3 cup	liquid honey	75 ml
1/2 tsp	nutmeg	2 ml
1/2 tsp	cinnamon	2 ml
	Juice of 1/2 lemon	

1 Preheat your oven to 350°F (180°C).

2 In a large skillet, heat the canola oil over a medium-high heat until very hot and almost smoking.

3 Pat the steaks dry with paper towel. Season with salt and fresh cracked pepper.

4 Pan-fry the steaks 3 at a time, for 2 minutes per side. Transfer to a warming plate and finish in the oven for 13 minutes for medium-rare.

5 Deglaze the pan with the blueberry vinegar, scraping up the juicy brown bits from the bottom and sides of the pan.

6 Transfer the vinegar mixture to a small saucepan and add the remaining ingredients. Bring to gentle simmer over a medium heat and cook until reduced to chutney consistency. Transfer to a bowl and set aside to cool.

For the blueberry poivrade:

"Sweating" is a cooking technique whereby veggies are gently cooked until soft but not browned and the juices, which are released by the heat, do not evaporate but rather are concentrated in the cooking fat. Think of it as a very gentle sautéing. It works very well with mushrooms or shallots in a bit of butter.

3	shallots, diced	3
1/2 cup	good red wine	125 ml
1/4 cup	blueberry vinegar	50 ml
1 tsp	fresh cracked pepper	5 ml
3 cups	strong beef stock	750 ml
3 cups	chicken stock	750 ml
	Salt, to taste	
1 cup	cold unsalted butter, cut into cubes	250 ml

1 In a medium saucepan, sweat the shallots over a medium-low heat for 3 minutes or until soft. Add the wine and vinegar and bring to a gentle boil over a medium-high heat. Reduce heat and simmer until reduced by three-quarters, about 15 minutes or so.

2 Add the pepper, stock, and chicken stock to the pot and return to a boil. Reduce the heat once again and simmer until reduced by half. Season to taste with salt and additional fresh cracked pepper.

3 Whisk in chilled butter 1 cube at a time until desired taste is achieved. Trust your taste buds.

To serve:

1 Remove the steaks from the oven. On a cutting board, slice each steak lengthwise against the grain into 5 or 6 slices.

2 Cover the face of each serving plate with some of the poivrade. Fan the slices out on each plate, with the closed end of the fan facing into the middle of the plate.

3 Place a slice of the croquette at the point of the fanned steak slices. Top the croquette with some of the chutney.

4 Garnish with any leftover fresh blueberries and fresh herb sprigs. *Voilà!*

"As for butter versus margarine, I trust cows more than chemists."
Joan Gussow

Here's a tip. If you are ever going to film a story involving Her Majesty the Queen of England and don't want to spend a lot of time being frisked by burly undercover Mounties, don't say "we're here to shoot the Queen"!

We have encountered many an obstacle in putting stories together for the show, but none like the time Queen Elizabeth came to the colonies in the summer of 1997. Prime Minister Chrétien was to host the only public dinner for Her Majesty at the venerable Royal York Hotel in Toronto and we simply *had* to get into the kitchens there.

First of all, we had submit our request to Buckingham Palace, which turned us down flat because of recent negative "reporting" about the Queen's eating habits while on vacation somewhere in Europe. After much help from the Department of Foreign Affairs (honest to God, there's this poor guy there whose life we made miserable) and numerous back-and-forth fax transmissions assuring the Brits that we had nothing but good intentions, we were finally granted permission to film the dinner. On certain conditions. One, we would not attempt to interview anybody associated with the Queen's visit. Two, we couldn't film Her Majesty eating.

Apparently it is untoward for the Queen of England to be caught on film with spinach between her teeth.

No biggie, because we were more interested in the behind-the-scenes preparations for the big meal than in the actual eating thereof. If ever you have occasion to stay at the Royal York (and you should, because it is a wonderful hotel with atmosphere and old-world charm up the yin-yang), ask Nancie Hall, super PR goddess, for a tour of the kitchens. We've shot in a lot of great places, but nothing comes close to the Royal York. Its kitchens are on four floors, and you could play football in them. The process moves from prep on the lower floors to finishing plates just as they go out the door on this really cool culinary conveyor belt.

The meals for the head table that night were made personally by expat Scotsman Executive Chef George McNeil and his hand-picked lieutenants, with the help of a shadowy guy in a dark suit who would bag little bits of the meal and drop them into dry ice for analysis (we're not kidding, folks). The best of the best in Royal York staff were on hand to serve and we were privy to a virtual ballet of food, wine, and service.

The following dishes were actually served to the Queen, the prime minister, and their 900 guests that evening (don't worry, we scaled the recipes down so you can make them for six people).

Grilled Breast of Chicken Filled with Oka Cheese and Fresh Sage

Serves 6 as a main course

6	chicken breasts, bone in and skin on	6
	Salt and freshly cracked pepper	
6 tbsp	olive oil	90 ml
6	large sage leaves	6
6	Oka cheese slices, about 1 x 3 x 1/2 inches/ 2.5 x 7.5 x 1 cm thick	6

1 Preheat your oven to 350°F (180°C). Season the chicken breasts with salt and fresh cracked pepper.

2 Heat 2 tbsp (30 ml) of olive oil in a large non-stick skillet over a medium-high heat. Add 2 of the chicken breasts to the oil once it's hot and pan-sear on all sides until golden brown. Use tongs or a spatula when turning the chicken, as you want to avoid piercing the skin. You're not trying to cook the chicken through, only to brown it on the outside, so don't cook it too long. When the first 2 chicken breasts are done, transfer them to a large plate to cool and repeat the process with the remaining breasts.

3 Once the chicken breasts are cool enough to handle, you're going to make a pocket between the meat and the skin to insert the sage and the cheese. Be very careful not to tear holes in the skin or the cheese will ooze out while baking in the oven. Try gently slipping the handle of a soup spoon in and carefully move it about so that it separates the skin from the meat. With a little practice you'll be able to do it with your fingers.

4   Place a sage leaf on top of each cheese slice. Insert the sage and cheese combo into the pocket you've made, cheese-side-up. Place the chicken breasts on a large baking sheet and cook in the middle of the oven for 20 to 25 minutes. Remove the chicken from the oven and let them sit for 5 minutes before serving.

5   Serve with bulgur wheat and wild rice risotto and sour apricot juice (recipes and plating directions follow).

Bulgur Wheat and Wild Rice Risotto with Woodland Mushrooms

1 cup	bulgur wheat, picked over	250 ml	**Serves 6 as a main course**
	Salt and freshly cracked pepper		
3 quarts	chicken stock	3 L	
1 cup	wild rice, picked over	250 ml	
1/2 lb	shiitake mushrooms	225 g	
1/2 lb	oyster mushrooms	225 g	
1/2 lb	cremini (brown) mushrooms	225 g	
6 tbsp	olive oil	90 ml	
2 tbsp	chopped garlic	30 ml	
1	medium onion, diced	1	
1 cup	arborio rice	250 ml	
1/2 cup	dry white wine	125 ml	
1/2	bunch fresh thyme, picked	1/2	
1/2	bunch fresh chives, chopped	1/2	
2 tbsp	butter	30 ml	
3 tbsp	grated Parmesan cheese	45 ml	

1   In a large saucepan, combine bulgur wheat, a pinch of salt, and 3 cups (750 ml) of the chicken stock over medium-high heat. Bring to a boil and reduce the heat. Simmer until the wheat feels tender and tested, about 12 to 15 minutes. Once cooked, drain the stock off and set the wheat aside.

2   Add the wild rice, a pinch of salt, and 4 cups (1 L) of the chicken stock to a saucepan and bring to a boil over a medium-high heat.

3   Reduce heat and simmer until the wild rice grains have exploded and feel tender when eaten. The time this takes will vary considerably, depending on the freshness and quality of the rice you use, so pay attention after 15 to 20 minutes. Once the rice has

cooked, drain off the chicken stock and set the rice aside with the wheat.

4   Pull stems from the caps of the shiitake mushrooms. Throw the stems away. Blah . . . they're tough and stringy and inedible. Slice the caps into thirds.

5   Pull the stems off the oyster mushrooms and discard the stems. Pull the caps into strips.

6   Slice up all the brown mushrooms, stems on. Set all the mushrooms aside in one bowl.

7   In a second skillet, add 3 tbsp (45 ml) of the olive oil over a medium heat. Add the garlic and 2 tbsp (30 ml) of the onion and sauté for 2 minutes. Add all the mushrooms and continue to sauté until mushrooms are soft, about 3 or 4 minutes.

8   In the same pan as you did the bulgur wheat and wild rice, add the remaining olive oil and onion and sauté for 3 minutes over a medium heat. Add the arborio rice and the mushroom mixture. Blend well and continue to cook for 2 minutes.

9   Add white wine to rice and mushrooms and stir well. Add 2 cups (500 ml) of the chicken stock and continue to stir.

10   Stir rice often as it cooks to prevent it sticking to the bottom of the pan. Add another 2 cups (500 ml) of the chicken stock when the first batch has almost bubbled away and been absorbed by the rice.

11   After the second batch of stock is almost gone, taste the rice to see if it is done. It should be tender with just a little al dente snap in the middle. If it isn't ready, add a little more stock and continue to cook, checking the consistency on a regular basis.

12   Once the arborio rice is done, fold in the wild rice, bulgur wheat, thyme, and chives. Mix well and then incorporate the butter and Parmesan cheese, stirring all the while. Adjust taste with salt, fresh cracked pepper, and more grated cheese, if necessary. If the risotto is too sticky, then add a touch of chicken stock you've nuked for 3 minutes till you reach a desired consistency.

13   Let sit covered for a few minutes before serving so that the flavours might properly blend.

Sour Apricot Juice

1 tbsp	olive oil	15 ml
1	small onion, finely diced	1
14 fl oz	canned apricots	398 ml
2 tbsp	dry white wine	30 ml
2 tbsp	apricot brandy	30 ml
2 tbsp	sherry vinegar	30 ml
1 1/2 cups	chicken stock	375 ml
1 tbsp	unsalted butter	15 ml

Salt and freshly cracked pepper, to taste

Makes 1 cup of sauce

1 In a medium saucepan, heat olive oil over medium heat.
2 Add onion and sauté for 4 minutes. Add the apricots and sauté for 3 minutes.
3 Add white wine, apricot brandy, and sherry vinegar. Let the mixture simmer for 2 minutes or so, until reduced by half.
4 Add the chicken stock and reduce heat. Let the sauce simmer for 12 to 15 minutes.
5 Add butter and blend using a hand blender until the apricots have been puréed and the sauce is smooth.
6 Season with salt and fresh cracked pepper to taste. If the sauce is a bit too sweet from the apricots, then add a bit more sherry vinegar until you get the desired level of acidity.
7 Pass the sauce through a fine sieve to give the sauce a clean finish.
8 To serve, place a large serving spoonful of the risotto in the middle of the plate. Lean one of the chicken breasts against the rice and spoon the sauce around them. Add fresh thyme sprigs planted into the risotto for garnish.

Chocolate and Roasted Walnut Tart with Caramelized Peaches and Raspberry Sorbet

Want a laugh? Go to any grocery store in Europe and ask for corn syrup. Then watch as they patiently explain that you can't get syrup from corn...

Makes one 11-inch tart

For the chocolate and roasted walnut tart:

2 cups	corn syrup	500 ml
4 tbsp	dark chocolate	60 ml
1/2 cup	granulated sugar	125 ml
5	whole eggs	5
1 tbsp	melted unsalted butter	15 ml
Approximately 1 lb	walnut crumbs	450 g

1 Preheat your oven to 350°F (180°C).
2 In a medium saucepan, warm the corn syrup over a low heat and add the dark chocolate. Melt together and remove from heat. Allow the mixture to cool slightly.
3 Add sugar and eggs to the syrup mixture and combine well. Add the melted butter.
4 Pour the mixture into an 11-inch (27.5-cm) pastry flan and sprinkle the walnut crumbs evenly over the entire tart.
5 Bake in the middle of the oven for 35 minutes.
6 Remove the tart from the oven and allow to cool on a baking rack. To serve, slice the tart and spoon some caramelized peaches on each piece. Put a scoop of sorbet on the side and enjoy.

For the caramelized peaches:

2	peaches	2
1–2 tbsp	sugar	15–30 ml

1 Halve and pit the peaches, leaving the skin on.
2 Cut each peach half into thirds.
3 Sprinkle the peach slices with the sugar.
4 Heat a non-stick pan over a medium-high heat.
5 Put the peach slices into the hot pan, and sear them quickly on both sides, and remove to cool.

For the raspberry sorbet:
Whaddaya nuts? Go buy some excellent sorbetti or gelato or frozen yoghurt to serve with this dessert.

The Canadian VQA

Galileo once said that wine is like water held together by sunlight. It is the stuff of dreams and poetry. From wine comes passion, from passion comes dreams, from dreams come poetry. A good glass of the grape unleashes a flood of sensations that no other food or nectar can produce.

By now, you've probably figured out we have little patience for the snobbery and pretence that often muddles the enjoyment of good food. This goes double for wine. It's fermented grape juice, for God's sake! We sniff at sniffing the cork! We wonder why it's so intimidating to enjoy one of life's great simple pleasures. So when we went to do a story about Canadian wines, we decided to use the occasion to debunk, demystify, and denounce much of the hoity-toityness surrounding the grape. Here's what we think:

Dollar for dollar, Canadian wine is as good as the French or the Italian or the South African or the Californian stuff. Yes, there are some incredible wines from abroad that we can't match, but they're 200 bucks a bottle and you'd be afraid to drink them anyway. The Canadian wine industry has come a long way in the last 20 years. From oversized jugs favoured by frat house sangria parties and your finer rubbies to international award winners, Canadian wines now hold their own on the international tasting circuit.

Recently, Canadian wineries have tried to bring some order to their business by introducing the VQA (Vintner's Quality Assurance) label on those bottles that meet a minimum standard of production. VQA does not always ensure a good-tasting bottle of wine, but it's a good start. The wineries of southern Ontario produce about 80 percent of Canada's wine output and, on the whole, we find their whites better than their reds. British Columbia, on the other hand, has incredible reds and whites but many of the vineyards are so small that often a handful of restaurants snap up their entire yields every year. Too bad for us.

The other thing to consider is that to be a winemaker in Canada means to be a bit of a non-conformist, so many great vineyards have opted out of VQA labelling on principle, including fab vinos from Quebec and Nova Scotia. But all in all, your $15 Canuck vino is a pretty good buy for any dinner table.

Please remember this: Above all, do not let anybody tell you what is or is not a good bottle of wine. If you like the taste, buy the wine and drink it to your good health.

Here then are some of our favourite wine-based recipes that feature the complexity of tastes one can get out of a bottle of wine and nowhere else.

Braised Short Ribs with Roasted Red Pepper and Red Wine Sauce

Braising is the simple no-fuss process of cooking meats and vegetables for a longer period of time at a lower heat. Braising gives you extraordinary flavour, and the long cooking time breaks down the fibrous content of less expensive meats. Short ribs are often overlooked as a meat course. They are quite inexpensive and, when braised, the meat is tender and juicy and falls away from the bone...mmmm. The roasted red pepper in the wine sauce adds an extra zip. This is a meal that tastes complicated and rich but is very easy to make. Because you just stick the pan in the oven when braising, it leaves you time to do other things. As always, go to a good butcher for your ribs. Enjoy.

Serves 6 as a main course

2	beef short ribs (5 1/2 lbs/2.75 kg each)	2
	Salt and freshly cracked pepper	
3	14-oz/398 ml cans tomatoes, chopped and peeled	3
8	carrots, peeled and coarsely chopped	8
3	celery stalks, coarsely chopped	3
3	large onions, coarsely chopped	3
1	bunch parsley	1
8	garlic cloves	8
3	sprigs fresh rosemary (or 2 tbsp/30 ml dried)	3
1 tbsp	dried sage	15 ml
1 tbsp	black peppercorns	15 ml
4	bay leaves	4
1 1/2	bottles good red wine	1 1/2
5–6 cups	water	1.25–1.5 L
2	large red peppers, roasted, skin removed, and cut into slices	2

1 Preheat your oven to 500°F (260°C).
2 Arrange ribs in 1 layer on a foil-lined baking sheet and season with lots of salt and fresh cracked pepper.
3 Roast the ribs in the middle of the oven for about 30 minutes or until they have browned. Reduce heat to 325°F (160°C).
4 Place the ribs and all their juices in a large ovenproof pot. Add the

other ingredients, except for the roasted red peppers, to the pot. Add just enough water to cover the ribs completely.

5   Cover the pot tightly and cook in the middle of the oven for about 3 hours. Meanwhile, rent a good movie or make love to your favourite sous-chef.

6   Remove the pot from the oven and immediately skim off any fat and foam that might have bubbled to the surface. Watch out you don't burn yourself on the rim of the pot!

7   Put the ribs in a large baking pan and set aside.

8   Strain the sauce through a fine sieve into a saucepan and bring to a boil over a high heat. Reduce heat to medium-high and simmer until the sauce has reduced to about 2 cups (500 ml), roughly 1 hour.

9   Add the red pepper to the sauce and purée until smooth.

10 Pour the sauce over the ribs and cook in the middle of the oven for about 30 minutes.

11 Arrange the ribs in the middle of each plate and pour the sauce over them. Serve with pan-roasted potatoes (recipe follows) placed around the ribs.

Tin Foil... Which Side Is Up?

Ever wonder whether it's the shiny or dull side of the tin foil that keeps in the heat or should be face-up when you're cooking? Turns out it doesn't make any difference at all! The texture of the foil is a function of the manufacturing process and has no effect on cooking or baking.

Pan-Roasted Potatoes

You can boil and cool the potatoes in advance. They taste best when pan-roasted at the last minute so that they hit the plate crispy and hot.

Serves 6 as a side dish

2 1/2 lbs	small new potatoes, skins on	1 kg
	Salt	
4 tbsp	olive oil	60 ml
2 tbsp	finely chopped fresh thyme leaves	30 ml

1 Place the potatoes in a large pot. Fill the pot with cold water until potatoes are just covered and add salt. Bring the potatoes to gentle simmer and cook for about 15 minutes or until barely tender.
2 Drain the potatoes in a colander and cool completely.
3 In a medium skillet, heat 2 tbsp (30 ml) of the olive oil with 1 tbsp (15 ml) of the thyme leaves over a medium-high heat. Don't let the oil reach smoking point.
4 Cut the potatoes in half and add half of them to the pan, flat-side-down.
5 Pan-fry the potatoes until golden brown without disturbing them, about 5 minutes. Flip the potatoes over so that the rounded sides get covered in oil and thyme leaves, and pan-fry for another 3 minutes. Remove them from the pan and set aside in a covered warming pan.
6 Repeat with the rest of the spuds and serve right away.

Pan-Wilted Garlic Spinach

While this recipe calls for toasted pine nuts, you can easily substitute toasted sunflower seeds at a fraction of the cost. Please, please, please use fresh spinach if it's in season.

Serves 6 as a side dish

3 tbsp	olive oil	45 ml
3	garlic cloves, finely minced	3
1 1/2 lbs	spinach, washed and stems removed	675 g
3 tbsp	balsamic or red wine vinegar	45 ml
1/2 cup	toasted pine nuts	125 ml

1 Heat the olive oil in a large skillet over a medium heat and add the garlic. Sauté the garlic until it turns a light golden brown. Be sure not to burn it!
2 Add the spinach in handfuls and mix well. Continue to cook until the spinach just begins to wilt. Add the vinegar and pine nuts and sauté 2 minutes longer.

Chicken Breasts in Riesling Sauce

6	half chicken breasts, bone and skin removed	6
	Salt and freshly cracked pepper, to taste	
3/4 cup	unsalted butter	175 ml
1	large onion, diced	1
6	garlic cloves, finely diced	6
	Flour (preferably potato flour, for dredging)	
1 cup	Riesling	250 ml
1 cup	dried cranberries	250 ml
1/3 cup	balsamic or red wine vinegar	75 ml
1 tsp	dried thyme	5 ml
1 tsp	dried savory	5 ml
1 tsp	dried oregano	5 ml

While any white wine will do in a pinch, we strongly suggest Riesling for this one, as it has a really fruity kick to it.

Serves 6 as a main course

1 Preheat your oven to 350°F (180°C).
2 Trim the chicken breasts of any excess fat. Pat them dry and season with salt and fresh cracked pepper.
3 Melt 4 tbsp (60 ml) of the butter in a large skillet over a medium-high heat. Add the onion and garlic and sauté for about 7 minutes or until golden brown. Keep an eye on the heat so you don't burn the garlic or you'll have to start all over again. Transfer the onion and garlic to a bowl and set aside for now.
4 Lightly dredge the chicken in flour (preferably potato flour), shaking off any excess.
5 Melt 2 more tbsp (30 ml) of the remaining butter in the same skillet, add 3 of the chicken breasts, and cook for about 4 minutes per side over a medium-high heat until crispy brown and almost cooked through. Remove the chicken to a baking pan and repeat this step with the remaining chicken.
6 Transfer chicken breasts to the oven and cook for 10 minutes longer.
7 Meanwhile, add the onion mixture, Riesling, cranberries, vinegar, and herbs to the skillet and bring to a boil. Let it simmer for about 7 or 8 minutes. Whisk in remaining butter.
8 Plate the chicken on a bed of pan-wilted garlic spinach (see recipe above) and spoon sauce over top. Serve with your choice of spud.

Patting the Chicken

You'll notice that throughout the book we recommend patting dry your meat, fish, and poultry with paper towel before pan-frying. The reason is that if the meat is wet, even with its natural juices, the surface of the meat will steam and the nice crispy brown coating you're going for won't be able to form.

Stuffed Veal Shoulder Roast in White Wine Reduction

Oh boy, you're going to love this one. You can substitute chard or escarole for the baby spinach. Talk to your butcher about the actual roast you will use. In order of preference, there's a shoulder roast, loin roast, and leg roast, but all are delicious. Have your butcher debone, trim, and butterfly the roast for you. Explain that you want to stuff and roll the roast, as that will determine the butterflying process. What you want to end up with is a roast that's been flattened into a fairly large "sheet," about 3/4 inch (2 cm) thick and roughly 12 inches (30 cm) square (hey, we're dealing with a cut of meat here, so don't worry if it's not square – nature isn't supposed to be mathematically precise) that you roll like a jelly roll. It's also best to have your butcher thinly slice the proscuitto while you wait (as opposed to buying it in a vacuum pack) and then layer it between sheets of waxed paper . . . this makes it much easier to work with.

Serves 6 as a main course

6 tbsp	olive oil	90 ml
2	medium onions, diced	2
2	garlic cloves, diced	2
2	bunches fresh spinach, washed and stems removed	2
1/2 cup	dried cranberries	125 ml
1 1/2 cups	chicken stock	375 ml
2/3 cup	grated Parmesan cheese	150 ml
1/2 cup	bread crumbs	125 ml
1/2 cup	pine nuts	125 ml
2 1/2 lbs	veal roast	1 kg
3 tbsp	finely diced fresh rosemary	45 ml
	Salt and freshly cracked pepper	
18	thin slices proscuitto	18
1 cup	white wine	250 ml
	Juice of 1/2 lemon	

1 Heat 4 tbsp (60 ml) of the olive oil in a large deep-sided skillet (with a lid . . . you'll need it later) over a medium-high heat until ripples begin to form in the oil. Add the onion and sauté for about 5 minutes or until it begins to turn a golden brown. Add the garlic and reduce the heat to medium. Sauté for another 2 or 3 minutes. Add the spinach and toss with tongs so that the spinach is covered in the oil and has begun to wilt.

2 Add the cranberries and ½ cup (125 ml) of the chicken broth and return the heat to medium-high so that it begins to boil. Bubble away until the broth is almost gone. Add the Parmesan cheese, bread crumbs, and pine nuts to the spinach mixture and mix well. Turn the heat off and set the skillet aside.

3 Lay the veal out on overlapping sheets of plastic wrap you've put down on a clean work surface and pat dry with paper towels. Season the veal with the rosemary, salt, and fresh cracked pepper. Cover the entire face of the veal with the slices of proscuitto, overlapping the slices a bit (they'll probably come like that in the package anyway).

4 Spoon the spinach filling onto the proscuitto in a horizontal line along the end of the veal closest to you. Be sure to leave ½ inch

(1 cm) or so free of filling on all sides. Basically, you are about to make a giant veal spring roll. Don't worry if there's leftover stuffing, as you'll use it later. Fold the side of the veal closest to you over the filling and tuck it underneath. Use the plastic wrap as an aide in the process. Make sure you roll it up good and tight. Okay . . . keeeeeep rolling away from you until you have a big stuffed veal roll (just make sure you don't roll the plastic wrap into the meat). *Voilà!* Excellent! Sounded a lot harder than it was, right?

5 Tie the roast up every inch or so with kitchen string, and then tie it once horizontally across the roast. Season with salt and fresh cracked pepper.

6 Heat the remaining olive oil in the same skillet you used to make the stuffing over a medium-high heat and brown the veal roast on all sides until a nice crispy golden-brown exterior is achieved, about 4 minutes per side. And don't forget to stand it on its two ends to brown as well. It's easy to do if you hold it up using tongs.

7 Once the roast has browned, pour in the wine and remaining stock and bring to a gentle simmer. Reduce the heat to low, cover the skillet, and cook for 20 minutes. Turn the roast over and cook for another 20 minutes. Remove the roast from the pan and tent with tin foil to keep warm.

8 Turn the heat up to high and bring the wine and stock mixture to a boil. Scrape up all the brown bits stuck to the bottom and sides of the skillet. Continue to reduce for 10 minutes and strain through a fine sieve. Add the lemon juice and cover to keep warm.

9 To serve, remove the string from the roast and slice it into 12 slices. Place 2 slices on each serving plate and drizzle with the sauce. Serve with Rosemary-Parmesan Mashed Potatoes (see Chapter 11) or Pan-Roasted Potatoes (see recipe above) and lemon grilled zucchini (see Chapter 1) or asparagus.

The Culinary Grand Prix at Whistler

Carlo Rota is not just the host of *The Great Canadian Food Show*, he is also a good friend and avid aficionado of all things good and tasty in the world (read into that whatever you will). Carlo lacks one thing that most great actors have . . . a monstrous ego. Carlo spins his on-camera magic and when the director yells, "Cut, next scene," he grabs some gear and humps it back to the van. There have been more than one 20-hour shooting days, when he has been asleep on his feet. But he always sucks it up when the camera rolls. Gotta love this guy.

So when we approached Carlo with the idea that he compete against 10 crack professional chefs *and* in real time (45 minutes) *and* in front of an audience (500 people) *and* without any foreknowledge of what ingredients he would be working with, he, of course, said, "Sure."

This episode took place at the wonderful Chateau Whistler (which is a very fortunate name for the hotel, as it is in Whistler), and the Culinary Grand Prix was put on as a charity fundraiser. Poor Carlo. All that these other guys (who cook every day for a living) had to do was commence cookin'. Carlo also had the small responsibilities of carrying a television episode, delivering his lines, bantering, acting like he's having fun, and playing to the two cameras filming him! That he was even able to finish his dish was a miracle.

Here are some recipes inspired by the dishes created that night.

Pork and Asparagus–Stuffed Parmesan Baskets

1 1/4 cups	grated Parmesan cheese	300 ml
3 tbsp	unsalted butter	45 ml
Approximately 1 lb	pork tenderloin, trimmed	450 g
	and cut into 1/2-inch/1-cm medallions	
	Salt and freshly cracked pepper, to taste	
2	carrots, peeled and finely diced	2
12	asparagus spears, trimmed and	12
	cut into 1/2-inch/1-cm pieces	
1 tsp	finely diced lemon rind	5 ml

1 Heat a small non-stick skillet over medium heat. Watch out: not too hot!

2 Add 3 tbsp (45 ml) of the Parmesan cheese to the skillet in an even layer. Let it melt on its own for about 2 minutes. It's like making caramel: Resist the temptation to stir it!

3 Using a plastic spatula, carefully turn the cheese over as you would a pancake. Let it cook for 1 or 2 minutes until it begins to firm up, but before it browns. It should still be soft and pliable.

4 Get a bowl that holds about 2 cups (500 ml) and lightly oil the outside of it with olive oil. Removing the skillet from the stove, slide the cheese over the inverted bowl and gently press down on it so that it moulds to the bowl's shape. Let the cheese cool and harden. Gently turn the bowl over onto paper towel until it's right-side-up. The cheese basket should separate easily.

5 Repeat the process with the remaining cheese. This can be done hours in advance of your meal.

6 In the same skillet, melt 1 tbsp (15 ml) of butter. Season the tenderloin medallions with salt and freshly cracked pepper and pan-fry half of them over medium heat for 3 minutes per side. Remove the pork from the skillet. Add 1 tbsp (15 ml) of butter and repeat the process with the rest of the pork. Set aside to cool.

7 Add the remaining butter to the skillet and sauté the carrots and asparagus over medium-high heat for about 4 minutes or until the asparagus is al dente. Add the lemon rind and sauté for 30 seconds.

8 Dice the pork medallions and add to the asparagus mixture.

9 Place 1 Parmesan basket on each small serving plate, spoon in one-sixth of the asparagus and pork mixture, and serve with lemon wedges or topped with an edible flower.

This was a fun recipe to make and it takes no time whatsoever. The recipe actually calls for a bit more Parmesan than you need, in case your first basket doesn't turn out. Don't worry if they don't look like perfect baskets; every basket should look different and a bit wobbly. If we wanted everything to be perfect and the same, we'd get a machine to do it. As always, use the best Parmesan possible for the tastiest dish.

Serves 6 as a starter

Chilled Smoked Salmon Soup with Chive Oil

Possibly the most elegant soup we've ever come across. It is a wonderful starter for a chi-chi-la-la summer dinner party or to bring to a backyard potluck.

Serves 6 as a starter

1	bunch chives, washed and coarsely chopped	1
1/2 tsp	white pepper	2 ml
1/2 cup	canola oil	125 ml
6 tbsp	unsalted butter	90 ml
6	shallots, finely diced	6
3	garlic cloves, finely diced	3
Approximately 1/2 lb	smoked salmon, coarsely chopped	225 g
3 tbsp	flour	45 ml
3 cups	chicken stock	750 ml
	Juice of 1 lemon	
2	bay leaves	2
2 cups	35% cream	500 ml

1 Purée the chives, white pepper, and canola oil and set aside. You can make it a day in advance and keep it in the fridge if you want.

2 Melt the butter in a soup pot over medium-high heat and add the shallots and garlic. Sauté for 3 minutes and add the smoked salmon. Mix well and sauté for 2 minutes.

3 Sprinkle the flour over top and mix well. Continue to sauté, stirring now and then, for 1 or 2 minutes until the flour binds to the salmon mixture.

4 Pour in the chicken stock while stirring and bring to a boil. Reduce the heat and simmer at a gentle boil for 10 minutes. Add the lemon juice and bay leaves and stir. Simmer for 10 minutes. Remove the pot from the heat and let it cool for a bit.

5 Remove the bay leaves and purée the soup until liquid. Don't worry that there are chunks floating in it. Get a large container (like a big Tupperware container) and strain the soup through a fine sieve. You're going to have to do this in batches, using a spoon to scoop the solids around and push the trapped liquid through the sieve. At the end of every batch you strain, you'll be left with a lump of smoked salmon solids in the sieve. Throw it out and repeat with the next batch.

6 Add the cream to the strained soup and mix well. Cover and refrigerate for at least 3 hours or preferably overnight.

7 To serve, divide the soup among 6 serving bowls. Take 1 tbsp (15 ml) of the chive oil and hold the spoon about 6 inches (15 cm)

over one of the bowls. Let the oil drip off the end of the spoon in splotches. It will hit the soup surface and fan out in mini chive-oil explosions. Very cool. Serve immediately.

Steak and Frites with Honey-Buttered Carrots

1/3 cup	unsalted butter	75 ml
6	big juicy steaks, rib-eyes or sirloins, each about 1 inch/2.5 cm thick	6
	Salt and freshly cracked pepper	
2 tbsp	finely diced fresh rosemary	30 ml
6	large baking potatoes	6
12	fresh carrots, peeled and quartered	12
6 tbsp	liquid honey	90 ml
	Vegetable oil (for deep-frying)	
	Fresh rosemary twigs (for garnish)	
1	big-screen television (preferably with picture-in-picture capabilities)	1

1 Nuke 2 tbsp (30 ml) of the butter for 20 seconds or until melted. Pat the steaks dry and brush them with the melted butter. Season with salt and fresh cracked pepper. Sprinkle the rosemary onto the steaks and rub in. Let stand at room temperature.

2 Peel the potatoes and cut them into ¼-inch (0.5-cm) strips so that they look like little mini 2x4 sheets of plywood. Soak them for 15 minutes in a large bowl filled with ice water. The water will turn milky white as the starch is drawn out of the potatoes.

3 While the potatoes are soaking, place the carrots in a large non-stick skillet with ½ cup (125 ml) of water and cover. Simmer over a medium-high heat for a few minutes until the water has almost completely evaporated. Add the honey and remaining butter to the skillet and cover again. Set aside for the moment.

4 When there are about 3 minutes left in the potato-soaking process, pour enough oil into a large skillet to reach 2 inches (5 cm) in depth. Heat the oil over a high heat until it reaches 325°F (160°C) on your candy thermometer. If you're going to do your steaks on the bar-b-que, now would be a good time to fire it up.

5 As soon as the 15 minutes are up, drain the potato slices in a

Here is your basic meat and potatoes dinner with a continental twist. The potatoes are done *à la frite* in the tradition of the best Belgian bistros (sorry, *mes amis*, we think the Belgians do frites better than the French!). These are the best gosh-darned fries you'll ever taste. The secret is in the ice-water bath and the double frying process. When you're done, let the oil cool and strain it into a plastic container for your next frying occasion. If you want to go really continental, then crumble 1 tsp (5 ml) of good-quality blue cheese (at room temperature) on top of the steaks just before serving. Substitute the same amount of maple syrup or half the amount of sesame oil for the honey for a different carrot on your plate. The big-screen television is an optional ingredient; we thought this would be the perfect excuse to get one...

Serves 6 as a main course

colander and pat them dry with paper towel . . . dry them really well. By this time the oil should have reached 325°F. Add the potatoes to the oil in 4 batches. You don't want to add too many potatoes at the same time or they'll drop the temperature of the oil so drastically that frying will become difficult and you'll end up with soggy spuds. Okay…so throw your first batch in and fry for about 2 or 3 minutes, until they're cooked through but before they begin to turn french-fry golden brown. Remove the potatoes with a slotted spoon or tongs and transfer to a bowl lined with paper towels. Meanwhile, the temperature of the oil should have returned to 325°F (160°C). Repeat the process with the remaining potatoes. Turn off the heat under the oil.

6 Place your steaks buttered-side-down on your bar-b-que grill. If you're cooking indoors, then go buttered side down over a medium-high heat in 2 skillets, so that you can cook the steaks all at once. You've got some nice cuts of meat there, so cook them for 3 or 4 minutes per side for medium-rare. When done, transfer the steaks to a large plate and tent with tin foil to keep warm.

7 Turn the heat back on under the frying oil and heat to 325°F (160°C).

8 Return the covered skillet with the honey-butter carrots to the stove-top and reheat over a medium-low heat.

9 Return the potatoes to the frying oil in 3 batches. Fry the spuds for an additional minute or until they start to get crispy and golden brown. Replace the paper towel in the bowl and transfer the newly fried potatoes to the bowl with tongs or a slotted spoon. Season with salt and fresh cracked pepper. Repeat the process with the remaining potatoes.

10 Place 1 steak on each plate and add the carrots and frites. Place a twig of fresh rosemary on top of each steak (unless you're going to add the cheese crumble) and serve. Blow a big raspberry at anyone who asks you for ketchup. Throw on some Edith Piaf (yeah, yeah, we know she's not Belgian, but she *is* great), pour a big legs-up-to-here red wine, and have everyone at the table tell a story about the best concert they've ever been to.

11 Later on, invite everyone to watch *The Great Canadian Food Show* in Carlovision on your new big-screen television.

Pork Tenderloin in a Cassis Sauce

3 cups	chicken stock	750 ml
3 cups	beef stock	750 ml
3	pork tenderloins (each about 1/2 lb/225 g)	3
	Salt and freshly cracked pepper	
	Flour (preferably potato flour, for dredging)	
2/3 lb	cold unsalted butter	300 g
1 1/2 cups	crème de cassis liqueur	375 ml
2/3 cup	red wine vinegar	150 ml
1 cup	dried currants	250 ml

1 Preheat your oven to 350°F (180°C).

2 Combine the chicken and beef stocks in a saucepan and bring to a boil over a high heat. Reduce heat to medium-high and simmer until reduced by half, about 30 minutes.

3 Trim the tenderloins of any excess fat and silver skin. Pat them dry and season with salt and fresh cracked pepper. Lightly dredge the tenderloins in flour (preferably potato flour), shaking off any excess.

4 Melt 4 tbsp (60 ml) of the butter in a large skillet over a medium-high heat. Place the tenderloins in the skillet and cook on all sides until a crispy brown exterior is achieved, about 8 minutes.

5 Remove the pork from the skillet and place in a baking pan. Place the pork in the middle of the oven and cook for 15 minutes.

6 Pour off the excess butter from the skillet and return it to the stove-top. Deglaze the pan by adding the crème de cassis liqueur and vinegar. Let the liquid bubble and scrape up all the juicy brown bits clinging to the sides and bottom of the pan. Let the liquid reduce by half, about 15 to 20 minutes.

7 By now the pork should be done. Remove from the oven and pour any juices into the sauce. Tent the pork with tin foil to keep warm.

8 Add the reduced stock combination and the dried currants. Bring to a gentle boil and reduce again for another 20 minutes or until you get a nice thick syrupy consistency. Whisk in the remaining butter 1 chunk at a time.

9 Mound a nice big spoonful each of mashed potatoes (see Chapter 11) and mashed yams side by side and touching in the middle of each plate. Cut the tenderloins into medallions and arrange slices on top of the potatoes and yams. Pour the cassis sauce over the whole lot so that it drizzles over the pork and down the sides of the yam and potato mountain onto the plate.

Cassis is a deep-purple black currant–flavoured liqueur popular in Europe. It is relatively inexpensive as liqueurs go, and a bottle is well worth the investment if you only make this dish twice a year for dinner parties. Again, this dish is relatively simple to prepare and pork tenderloin is one of the best buys meatwise on the market today. Three pork tenderloins (enough to serve six hungry people) shouldn't run you more than $12 or $14. Please don't go into cardiac arrest when you see how much butter is in the sauce. It works out to about 2 tbsp (30 ml) per person...come on, live a little! It's not like you're going to do this every night! This recipe calls for dried currants but dried cranberries work just as well in a pinch.

Serves 6 as a main course

Beef and Pork Stew

There are some dishes that seem to taste even better as leftovers, such as lasagna, chili, and stew. We've purposefully over-estimated the quantities here so that there will be lots left over for lunch the next day.

Serves 6, with leftovers

Approximately 1 lb	beef chuck, trimmed and cut into bite-size pieces	450 g
Approximately 1 lb	pork tenderloin, trimmed and cut into bite-size medallions	450 g
3 cups	dry red wine	750 ml
2	large leeks, washed and coarsely chopped, white parts only	2
2	large carrots, peeled and coarsely chopped into pieces the same size as the beef	2
2	turnips, peeled and coarsely chopped into pieces the same size as the beef	2
2	bay leaves	2
1	sprig fresh rosemary	1
1 tsp	dried thyme	5 ml
1 tsp	dried oregano	5 ml
6	garlic cloves, halved	6
2 tbsp	Worcestershire sauce	30 ml
3 tbsp	brandy or cognac	45 ml
6	bacon slices	6
	Salt and freshly cracked pepper	
	Flour (for dredging)	
2 cups	beef stock	500 ml
3	plum tomatoes, seeded and coarsely chopped	3

1 Combine the beef, pork, red wine, leeks, carrots, turnips, bay leaves, rosemary, thyme, oregano, garlic, Worcestershire sauce, and brandy in a large bowl and marinate at room temperature for 1 hour or overnight in the fridge.

2 Cook the bacon in a large pot over medium-high heat until crispy (*like we really need to tell you how to cook bacon!*). Transfer the pig strips to paper towel and set aside.

3 Remove the beef and pork from the marinade and pat dry with more paper towel. It's important that you get all the excess marinade off the surface of the meat, otherwise the flour won't cling properly. Reserve the marinade.

4 Season the beef and pork with salt and fresh cracked pepper and dredge in the flour, shaking off any excess. Brown the beef and

pork in the bacon fat over a medium-high heat until you get a nice golden-brown texture. Do this in 3 or 4 batches so that all the meat can brown without overcooking. If you run out of bacon fat between batches, add a little olive oil and heat it before going on to the next batch.

5 Once all the beef and pork has been browned and removed, you'll be left with some delicious brown bits clinging to the bottom of the pot. Pour in ½ cup (125 ml) of the marinade and bring to a boil. Scrape up all the brown bits and return the beef and pork to the pot.

6 Add the rest of the marinade, beef stock, and tomatoes and bring to a boil over a high heat. Reduce the heat so that the pot is gently simmering and cover. Cook the stew for 45 minutes. Remove the cover and give it a good stir and a taste test. Season to taste with salt and fresh cracked pepper and let it simmer for another 30 minutes or so without a lid.

7 To serve, cook enough egg noodles (or another pasta of your choice, but we really like egg noodles with this one) to feed 6 and toss the noodles with a bit of olive oil and some chopped fresh parsley. Plate the noodles and spoon the stew on top. Ladle some of the gravy over the stew and top with gremolata (see recipe in Chapter 8).

The Pelican Grill and Kitchen Jim

Jim Foster is our official fishmonger and the host of our "Kitchen Jim" columns. Jim and his partner, Marc, own the Pelican Fishery in an unassuming little strip mall in the south end of Ottawa. A couple of years ago they opened a small restaurant adjacent to the fish store and called it The Pelican Grill. The Grill serves the best fish and chips we've ever eaten, with a homemade tartar sauce to die for. Fresh, perfect seafood served simply is what makes Jim's restaurant a neighbourhood hit.

But Jim is more than just a guy who schleps fish for a buck. He is the father of three wonderful boys, a friend, and an involved member of his community. We cannot ever remember seeing Jim in a bad mood. With his aw-shucks Tom Hanks quirky good looks and his big toothy grin, he's the kind of guy you take to immediately. He knows his *poissons* and will gladly spend time with you explaining the differences in some of the varied catches displayed on his ice trays.

We're very lucky to have Jim Foster as our fishmonger, just as we are fortunate to have known dozens of other people in shooting *The Great Canadian Food Show* who have the same love of life, family, and what they do as our pal Jim does. Canada is chockablock with wonderful people who make their living from some aspect of the Canadian food experience. Maybe your Jim is a baker or a butcher or a grocer.

Here are a selection of recipes from The Pelican Grill and from dinner parties we've had with Jim and his beautiful wife, Joanne.

Leek and Mussel Soup

2 cups	water	500 ml
1 cup	dry white wine	250 ml
1 tsp	dried thyme	5 ml
1 tsp	dried sage	5 ml
1	bay leaf	1
1 3/4 lbs	fresh mussels, scrubbed and picked over	800 g
6	bacon strips	6
2 tbsp	unsalted butter	30 ml
2	garlic cloves, diced	2
5	medium leeks, white parts only, coarsely chopped and washed	5
Approximately 1 lb	russet or Yukon Gold potatoes, peeled and chopped	450 g
1	bottle clam juice	1
1 cup	35% cream	250 ml

This is definitely a special-occasion soup for when you really want to impress your guests. It's not hard to make, but it takes a bit of time, so save this one until you have a Saturday afternoon to work on it. This is a big hearty soup that cries out to be sopped up with good bread, and is therefore quite filling. It would go great with a lighter main course.

Serves 6 as a starter

1 Bring the water, white wine, thyme, sage, and bay leaf to a boil in a soup pot over high heat. Add the mussels and cook, covered. Bubble away for 5 minutes. Transfer the mussels to a large bowl using tongs or a slotted spoon and discard any that didn't open. Once the mussels have cooled enough to handle, remove them from their shells and set the meat aside. Throw out the shells.

2 The liquid in which you boiled the mussels has now been infused with a wonderful seafood flavour that has blended with the wine and herbs. Strain it through a fine sieve and set aside.

3 Add the bacon to the same soup pot and fry over medium heat until crispy. Remove the bacon and transfer to a plate lined with paper towels.

4 Add the butter to the pot and turn the heat up to medium-high. Once the butter has melted, add the garlic and leeks and sauté for 5 minutes or until tender. Toss in the potatoes and the wine liquid and turn the heat up to high. Get the whole thing boiling and cover the pot. Reduce the heat to medium so that it simmers away for a good 20 minutes or so until the potatoes are tender.

5 Add the clam juice and purée with a hand mixer, or cool the soup and purée in a blender. You can now set the soup aside until you're ready to serve.

6 To serve, reheat the soup over medium heat and add the mussels. Cook for a few minutes until warmed through, but be careful not

to let it come to a boil. Add the cream and stir thoroughly. Cook for 1 or 2 minutes until heated through without boiling.

7 Divide the soup among the 6 serving bowls, being sure to scoop to the bottom of the pot so that everyone gets some of the mussels. Crumble a slice of bacon over each bowl and serve with a warm baguette or crusty French bread.

P.E.I. Mussels with Cherry Tomatoes, Herbs, and Cream

If you can't get P.E.I. mussels, at least make sure they are fresh and Canadian! We would strongly recommend that you never ever buy mussels in one of those little mesh bags. Go see a fishmonger, who will pick out as many as you need from a large ice-filled basin. That way you know all the mussels are alive and fresh when you purchase them. Discard any that open before you cook them and any that remain closed after cooking.

If cherry tomatoes are out of season, substitute 4 plum tomatoes that have been cored and coarsely chopped.

Serves 6 as a starter

6 tbsp	olive oil	90 ml
4	plum tomatoes	4
1	medium onion, coarsely chopped	1
3	garlic cloves, coarsely chopped	3
7	shallots, coarsely chopped	7
3 1/2 lbs	fresh P.E.I. mussels, washed and picked over	1.5 kg
2 tbsp	chopped fresh thyme (or 1 tsp/5 ml dried)	30 ml
1 1/2 cups	good dry white wine	375 ml
6 tbsp	35% cream	90 ml
24	cherry tomatoes	24

1 In a large soup pot, heat the olive oil over medium-high heat and add the tomato, onion, garlic, and shallots. Sauté for 4 minutes, stirring constantly.

2 Add the mussels, cover the pot, and cook over high heat for 3 minutes.

3 Add the thyme and white wine. Cook uncovered for 2 minutes.

4 Add the cream and cook for 3 minutes. Discard any mussels that did not open.

5 Spoon the mussels and liquid into soup bowls. Add 4 cherry tomatoes to each bowl and serve immediately with fresh warmed baguette and unsalted butter.

*Pork and Asparagus-Stuffed
Parmesan Baskets*

Pork Tenderloin in a Cassis Sauce

*Steak and Frites with
Honey-Buttered Carrots*

*P.E.I. Mussels with Cherry Tomatoes,
Herbs, and Cream*

Chicken and Veggie Salad with Lemon Vinaigrette

Shrimp Flambé with Proscuitto

Pan-Seared Breast of Duck in
Soy-Honey Sauce

The Martooni Salad

Pelican Fuillette with Tarragon White Wine Sauce

3	half chicken breasts, deboned and skin removed	3
6	jumbo shrimp, peeled and deveined	6
1/2 cup	bay scallops	125 ml
1 tbsp	unsalted butter	15 ml
1 tbsp	olive oil	15 ml
1/2 cup	unsalted butter	125 ml
2/3 cup	finely diced Spanish onion,	150 ml
2	bunches fresh baby spinach, washed and stems removed	2
3/4 tsp	dried tarragon	3 ml
1 tbsp	chopped fresh thyme	15 ml
1/3 tsp	dried thyme	1.5 ml
	Juice of 2 lemons	
1/2 cup	35% cream	125 ml
	Salt and freshly cracked pepper, to taste	
2	sheets frozen puff pastry, thawed as per instructions on the box	2
2	egg yolks, separated from the egg whites and whisked	2

Serves 6 as a main course for Sunday brunch

1 Cut the chicken breasts into long thin slices. Dice the shrimp and drain the bay scallops.

2 In a medium fry pan, melt the 1 tbsp (15 ml) of butter over a medium heat and add the olive oil. Pan-fry the chicken strips for 4 minutes. Add the shrimp and scallops. Sauté for 1 minute longer. Transfer the ingredients to a bowl and set aside. Use the same pan for the next cooking step.

3 Preheat your oven to 500°F (260°C).

4 Melt the 4 oz (115 g) of butter over a medium heat in the previously used fry pan and sauté the onion for 3 minutes. Add the spinach and sauté 1 minute or until the spinach begins to wilt. Add the seafood and chicken mixture and sauté for another 6 minutes over a medium-high heat.

5 Add the tarragon, thyme, lemon juice, and 35% cream. Reduce heat to medium and blend thoroughly. Sauté for another 5 minutes. Season with salt and pepper.

6 Meanwhile, on a floured work surface, roll out the 2 sheets of puff pastry into 12-inch (30-cm) squares.

7 Place 1 sheet on a greased cookie sheet. Spoon the mixture onto the puff pastry, gently spreading evenly with the back of the spoon and leaving a 1-inch (2.5-cm) border around the edges.

8 Place the second puff pastry sheet on top of the first and crimp down the edges. Brush the top of the pastry with the egg yolk. Bake in the middle of the oven for about 12 minutes or until golden brown.

9 To serve, cut the pastry into 6 even squares and plate each square on a bed of mixed greens. Drizzle with the tarragon white wine sauce (recipe follows).

Tarragon White Wine Sauce

2 tbsp	unsalted butter	30 ml
1 tbsp	chopped fresh tarragon leaves (or 1/2 tsp/2 ml dried)	15 ml
	Juice of 1 lemon	
1 cup	good dry white wine	250 ml
1/2 cup	35% cream	125 ml

1 While the puff pastry is baking, melt the unsalted butter in a small saucepan over a medium heat. Add the tarragon and lemon juice and stir for 1 minute.

2 Increase heat to medium-high for 30 seconds and add the white wine. Bring to a boil and reduce the heat to medium. Simmer until the liquid has reduced by half, about 7 minutes or so.

3 Add the 35% cream and bring to a gentle boil again. Simmer for 2 minutes longer.

Cherrywood-Grilled Arctic Char with Roasted Apple Coulis

3	McIntosh apples, cored, peeled, and quartered	3
6	Arctic char fillets (about 1/2 lb/225 g each), skin on	6
3 tbsp	unsalted butter	45 ml
15–20	fresh mint leaves	15–20
	Salt and freshly cracked pepper, to taste	
3	red peppers, roasted with the skins removed*	3
1/3 cup	white wine	75 ml

* *The fastest and simplest way to roast a pepper is as follows: Preheat your oven to 500°F (260°C). Cut the pepper in half and remove the bitter white pulp and seeds. Cover the pepper with a little olive oil and bake, flat side down, until the skin is charred black. Remove the pepper halves from the oven and let cool. Peel off the blackened skin. That's it, that's all.*

You can purchase aromatic wood chips at a camping and outdoor equipment store or at a bar-b-que specialty retailer. This recipe calls for cherrywood, but dried grape vines, alderwood, etc., will do nicely as well.

Serves 6 as a main course

1 Soak 4 handfuls of the wood chips as per instructions on the packaging.
2 Preheat the bar-b-que to 500°F (260°C). Line the upper grill with a double sheet of tin foil.
3 Roast the apple quarters for about 10 minutes. Clean the grill thoroughly.
4 Toss the wood chips directly onto the coals. Place the char fillets on the grill skin-side-up and close the cover. Grill for about 4 minutes or until grill lines appear on the char meat and the fillet can be removed without breaking apart.
5 Using a spatula, transfer the char fillets to the foil-lined upper grill. Close the lid again and bake for a further 7 minutes.
6 While the char is baking, melt the unsalted butter in a small saucepan over a medium-high heat. Add the roasted apple quarters and sauté for 3 minutes.
7 Add the mint and a dash of salt and fresh cracked pepper. Sauté 2 minutes longer.
8 In a food processor or blender, purée the pale mixture with the roasted red peppers and the white wine.
9 To serve, place a large spoonful of mashed potatoes mixed with baby green peas in the centre of a plate. Place a char fillet, skin side down, on top and pour some of the coulis onto the plate around the mashed potatoes.

Super-Fast Mussels with Garlic and Herbs

We've called for one garlic clove per serving because we're crazy for the stinky rose. Adjust your garlic content up or down, depending on how much smoochin' you plan on doing that night.

Serves 6

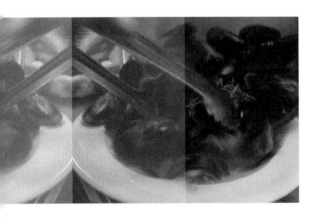

3 tbsp	olive oil	45 ml
6	shallots, finely diced	6
6	garlic cloves, coarsely chopped	6
1/2 cup	dry red wine	125 ml
1 1/2 cups	chicken stock	375 ml
2	plum tomatoes, cored, seeded, and coarsely chopped	2
1/2 tsp	freshly cracked pepper	2 ml
2 tbsp	freshly squeezed lemon juice	30 ml
1 tbsp	chopped fresh rosemary	15 ml
1–2 dashes	Tabasco or other quality hot sauce (optional)	1–2 dashes
4 1/2 lbs	mussels, cleaned and scrubbed	2 kg
1 tbsp	chopped fresh tarragon leaves	15 ml
1 tbsp	chopped fresh chives	15 ml

1 Heat the olive oil in a large soup pot over a medium heat and add the shallots and garlic. Cook until soft, stirring often and making sure not to burn the garlic or you're out of luck.

2 Add the vino and bring to a boil over a medium-high heat. Boil for 2 minutes, add the chicken stock, tomatoes, pepper, lemon juice, rosemary, and Tabasco (if desired), and continue to boil for another 2 minutes.

3 Add the mussels and cover the pot. Cook for 5 minutes. After 5 minutes, check the pot and remove any mussels that have opened. Transfer them to a bowl and continue to cook the rest of the mussels for another 5 minutes.

4 Remove the pot from the heat and discard any mussels that have not opened. Return the other mussels to the pot. Add the herbs and stir to mix well.

5 Divide the mussels between the serving dishes and ladle the sauce over top. Serve immediately with crusty bread and unsalted butter. Put Miles Davis on the stereo. Be cool.

Mussels in Coconut and Lime Nectar

2 tbsp	olive oil	30 ml
1	medium onion, halved and finely sliced	1
1	1-1/2-inch (4-cm) piece fresh ginger, peeled and finely diced	1
1 tbsp	ground turmeric	15 ml
3 1/2 lbs	mussels, cleaned and debearded	1.5 kg
2 cups	bottled clam juice	500 ml
1 1/2 cups	canned coconut milk	375 ml
3	plum tomatoes, halved, seeded, and coarsely chopped	3
3	hot peppers (such as jalapeño or Thai), halved, seeded, and finely diced	3
1 tbsp	grated lime peel	15 ml
	Juice of 3 limes	
1/2	bunch fresh coriander, stems removed and coarsely chopped	

We've made this one spicy, calling for three hot peppers, but you can adjust the level depending on your tolerance. Turmeric (of the ginger family) will give the dish a real zing and a powerful orangey colour. It can be bought really cheap at any bulk or health food store. Coconut milk is now available at most larger mainstream supermarkets. This is a dish best served with frosty cold beer chugged right out of the bottle (burping optional).

Serves 6

1 Heat the olive oil over a medium-high heat and add the onion. Cook for 4 minutes or until translucent. Add the ginger and turmeric and mix well. Stir for another minute or so. As the turmeric binds with the oil it will release an incredibly pungent aroma into your kitchen. It is a fabulous smell. Beat hungry persons back with a broom.

2 Add the mussels, clam juice, coconut milk, tomatoes, hot peppers, and lime peel to the pot and bring to a boil. Cover the pot and steam the mussels for 5 minutes. Remove opened mussels with a slotted spoon and continue to cook the remainder for another 5 minutes. Remove and discard any unopened mussels and return the open ones to the pot.

3 Stir in the lime juice and the coriander. Divide the mussels between the serving bowls and spoon the coconut-lime nectar over top. Serve immediately. Put some Don Ho on the stereo. Be cool.

Desserts are wonderful at The Pelican Grill. They're all homemade by uberdessertologist Katherine Boisvert, who works at The Grill and literally goes home at night and makes all the desserts for the restaurant. A lot of restaurant dessert recipes are fairly involved and require special equipment. We asked Katherine to supply us with two of her most popular recipes for you to try at home.

Key Lime Cheesecake Boisvert

You have to bake the crust. But the cheese-cake itself is a no-baker.

Makes one 9-inch tart

For the crust:

1 1/2 cups	graham cracker crumbs	375 ml
4 tbsp	sugar	60 ml
6 tbsp	unsalted butter, softened at room temperature	90 ml

1 Preheat your oven to 350°F (180°C).
2 Reserve ⅓-cup (80 ml) of the graham cracker crumbs for the topping and combine the rest in a bowl with the sugar and butter. Mix well.
3 Press the mixture onto the bottom and a bit up the sides of a 9-inch (22.5-cm) springform pan.
4 Bake in the middle of the oven for 6 minutes. Remove and set aside to cool.

For the filling:

2	envelopes of unflavoured gelatin	2
1 cup	fresh lime juice, about 5 limes' worth*	250 ml
1 1/2 cups	sugar	375 ml
5	large eggs, beaten	5
2 tsp	grated lime zest	10 ml
1 tsp	vanilla	5 ml
1 1/4 lbs	cream cheese, softened at room temperature	575 g
6 tbsp	unsalted butter, softened at room temperature	90 ml
2/3 cup	35% cream	150 ml
1/2 cup	lightly toasted coconut	125 ml

* *Want more juice from your lemons or limes? Cut them in half and nuke them on high for 1 minute before squeezing them. Also, insert a fork into the middle of the half and turn as you squeeze the juice out.*

1 In a medium saucepan, sprinkle the gelatin over the lime juice and let sit for 1 minute until softened. Stir over a low heat until the gelatin has dissolved.

2 Stir in the sugar, eggs, and lime zest. Increase heat to medium and cook for 7 minutes, stirring constantly. Whatever you do, don't let the mixture come to a boil or you're #@!#&***ed.

3 Stir in the vanilla. Remove from heat and cool slightly.

4 In a large mixing bowl, beat the cream cheese and butter with a mixer until smooth. Gradually beat in the gelatin mixture until well blended. Take your time. Refrigerate for 1 hour.

5 Whip the cream until stiff peaks appear. After the hour is up, fold the whipped cream into the cheese mixture. Pour the whole thing into the graham crust and spread evenly. Top with remaining graham cracker crumbs and toasted coconut.

Pecan Pumpkin Torte

For the torte:

1 1/4 lbs	vanilla wafers, crushed	575 g
1 cup	pecans, chopped	250 ml
3/4 cup	unsalted butter, softened at room temperature	175 ml
1	box spiced cake mix	1
1 1/4 lbs	canned pumpkin	575 g
5 tbsp	unsalted butter, also softened at room temperature	75 ml
4	large eggs	4

This is one of those occasions where using a canned food (the pumpkin) is well worth the time and hassle without compromising the quality of your dish whatsoever. This is a special-occasion cake that is actually quite easy to make. None of the steps are complicated; it just takes a bit of time. Set aside a Saturday afternoon for this recipe. Pour yourself a nice glass of wine or a cold frosty beer, put on some tunes, and enjoy yourself. Don't forget to let some deserving person lick the mixer blades once you've made the filling.

Makes enough for 12 to 16 servings

1 Preheat your oven to 350°F (180°C).

2 In a food processor, mix together the vanilla wafers, pecans, and ¾ cup (175 ml) of unsalted butter. Pulse on and off, stopping to scrape down the sides of the bowl every now and then, until blended and the mixture has formed into crumbs.

3 Press the crumbs evenly onto the bottoms of 3 greased and floured 9-inch (22.5-cm) round cake pans.

4 In the food processor combine the spiced cake mix, pumpkin, 5 tbsp (75 ml) butter, and the eggs. Process at a medium speed, stopping to scrape down the sides of the bowl every now and then, until well mixed and a batter consistency has been achieved.

5 Spread the batter evenly over the crumbs in all 3 of the pans and bake in the middle of the oven for 20 to 25 minutes or until a

toothpick inserted in the centre comes away cleanly. Remove from oven, do a pirouette (just seeing if you're paying attention), and cool for 5 minutes. Remove from the pans and cool completely.

For the filling:

3 cups	powdered sugar	750 g
Approximately 1/2 lb	unsalted butter, softened at room temperature	225 g
1/4 lb	cream cheese, softened at room temperature	115 g
2 tsp	vanilla	10 ml
1/4 lb	caramel topping	115 g
	Pecan halves (for garnish)	

1 In a small mixer bowl, combine the powdered sugar, unsalted butter, cream cheese, and vanilla. Using an electric mixer, beat at a medium speed until light and fluffy, scraping down the sides of the bowl often, about 3 minutes.

2 Lay one of the cakes nut-side-down onto a large serving plate. Top the cake with some of the filling. Place the second layer of cake nut-side-down on top of the filling. Slather with more filling and place the final layer of the cake on top. Do not put filling on top of the cake!

3 With the remaining filling, frost the sides of the cake only. Spread the caramel topping over the cake, allowing it to run down over the sides in a delicious, gooey mess. Arrange the pecan halves in rings around the top of the cake. Refrigerate immediately until topping has set.

Oyster Boy

20

Some men are born to oysters; others have oysters thrust upon them. This is the story of Chris Field, a man who for the better part of his life agitated nary a single brain cell in the consideration of *le baiser de la mer*, the sweet and salty oyster. This is the story of Oyster Boy.

Mr. Field, or Oyster Boy as he is known by one and all, is a man who knows his oysters. He speaks of these bivalves with their varied tastes and textures as a wine master would speak of grape varieties. He has shucked enough oysters that their shells, when stacked end to end, would likely reach the moon. Much to his wife's dismay, he has nicknamed his son "bivalve" (hey, it could be worse, he coulda called him "sea urchin"!). But it was not always so.

Although the exact details are murky, legend has it that, back in 1988, Chris Field was between jobs and living an oyster-free life in Toronto. One day, Chris was on his way to the Horseshoe Tavern and, stopping into a phone booth, found a mis-laid wallet. Being the decent sort that he is, Chris returned the wallet to its rightful owner. This act of honesty was to set Oyster Boy on a path that would alter his life forever. For the wallet belonged to none other than Rodney Clark, expat Maritimer and oyster impresario. Rodney was the man behind Rodney's Oyster Bar, a lovely raw bar that was the first to import a variety of fresh oysters for consumption on the half shell by urbane Torontonians, expense accounts at the ready. By way of a reward, Rodney offered our hero a dozen freshly shucked oysters and a job. And so it came to pass that Chris was initiated into the ways of the edible mollusc.

One does not immediately become a shucker at Rodney's, or indeed at any self-respecting raw bar. There is an apprenticeship in which one labours by busing tables, cleaning up, watching and learning, occasionally shucking, getting the technique down, and building up strength in the wrist and forearm. Gradually, Chris learned the secrets of the master shucker, the variations in technique required to open different types of oysters with one fell swish of the shucking blade.

Masterful oyster shucking is an art and a thing of beauty to behold. At Rodney's the shucker practises his craft under a halogen spotlight at the main raw bar. There, eager oyster consumers gather to watch the shucker pry open the bivalve and sever the meat from the attaching muscle in one fluid motion. Oyster after oyster, dozens becoming hundreds becoming millions, until the shucker is one with the oyster. It was there that Chris Field studied and learned his craft.

But one day, as it is with all students, it was time for Oyster Boy to leave his teacher. So he packed his things and made his way west in search of oyster fame and fortune. When we caught up with Chris, he was oystermeister in residence at the Crab Shack in Whistler, British Columbia, apparently the raw bar of highest elevation above sea level in all the Dominion, and possibly the world.

Nobody touches Chris's shucking knife. When not in use, it rests in a half lemon, like Excalibur waiting to be drawn from the stone. Chris's shucker is custom made. He had the safety guard removed for greater manoeuvrability and cut away half of the bulbous handle so that it sits flat in the palm of his hand. Next, he had the blade honed to a razor-sharp edge on the industrial grinder of an auto body repair shop. This is the tool of a professional.

And so if you should journey to Whistler in search of snow, sun, and fun, look up Oyster Boy. You'll find him most nights at the raw bar, his trusty shucking knife gleaming under the halogen spotlight as he shucks yet another dozen oysters. Get yourself a big cold frosty draught or some chilled white wine and pull up a stool in front of him. Casually ask Oyster Boy for a dozen on ice. He'll ask you what type of oyster you'd like. Reply by furrowing your brow and asking if there's really a difference. Watch Oyster Boy's eyes light up. Sit back, relax, take a long sip on your drink, and listen to a man truly in love with what he does regale you with stories of the bivalve. Cheers.

As for the oyster itself, we agree wholeheartedly with Mr. Field. There are most assuredly quite a range of tastes and textures in the selection of oysters available. Aficionados of the Atlantic oyster will tell you categorically that the Malpeque is the king of oysters. Meanwhile, on the Pacific Coast there are a number of worthy pretenders to the Mollusc Rex throne. Whether Pacific or Atlantic, oysters are one of the purest taste experiences there is. Eat 'em raw. Slurp 'em down. Savour the wonderful oyster liquid as it trickles down your throat, leaving behind a complex taste that is at once sweet and salty and positively overwhelms your tired taste buds.

While the best way to partake of an oyster is raw on the half shell, here are three other recipes for the bivalve we would recommend you give a shot. Check out Chapter 14 for Maritime Oyster Chowder as well.

Pan-Fried Oysters with Spicy Salsa

For the salsa:

1	plum tomato, seeded and diced	1
2 tbsp	diced red onion	30 ml
2 tbsp	seeded and diced English cucumber	30 ml
1	fresh hot pepper (such as Thai or jalapeño), seeded and finely diced	1
3 tbsp	fresh lime juice	45 ml
2 tbsp	chopped fresh coriander	30 ml

Combine all the ingredients in a small bowl and mix well.

For the oysters:

	Cornmeal or potato flour (for dredging)	
18	oysters, shucked and drained with 18 half shells set aside	18
	Vegetable oil (for frying)	

1 Put the cornmeal or potato flour in a plastic baggie.
2 Add 6 of the oysters to the cornmeal and shake the bag to coat the oysters.
3 In a large skillet, heat 1 ½ inches (4 cm) of vegetable oil until a cooking thermometer reads 375°F (190°C). Add the 6 oysters to the oil and fry for about 1 minute, turning with tongs, until the coating becomes a wonderful golden brown. Remove the oysters from the oil with a slotted spoon and drain on paper towel.
4 Repeat the process with the other oysters.
5 To serve, place 3 of the half shells on each serving plate. Mound a small spoonful of the salsa onto each shell and then place an oyster on top of the salsa. Garnish with additional coriander sprigs.

This is a great appetizer for those who can't face swallowing the bivalve raw. You get the fabulous sweet and spicy combo of the salsa followed by the crispy, salty taste of the fried oyster. Yum. The oysters should be slurped back as one would with the raw version. Make sure that the oil is very hot or the oysters won't fry properly.

Serves 6 as a starter

Skinny Oyster Po-Boy with Aioli and Chives

Oyster po-boy, or oyster loaf as it is some-times called, is a deep-fried delicacy of the working person's luncheon variety. Kinda like a lobster roll. We call this one "skinny" because we've substituted baked baguette slices for the more traditional full loaf one usually puts the oysters in. We think it also makes a wonderful appetizer if passed around on a large serving plate. The aioli we use is a variation on an old-world recipe from Provence. You can also use guacamole instead of or with the aioli for a really decadent taste. If you're worried about consuming raw eggs, use some prepared mayonnaise mixed with lemon juice, pepper, and Tabasco instead of the aioli, although it won't be as creamy in texture. If you do go with the guacamole, skip the red onion slice.

Serves 6 as a main course

For the aioli and chives:

4 tbsp	2% or homo milk	60 ml
4	garlic cloves, halved	4
2	egg yolks	2
1 cup	olive oil	250 ml
	Juice of 1/2 lemon	
8–10	chive stalks, diced	8–10
Dash	Tabasco, to taste	Dash
	Salt and freshly cracked pepper	

For the oysters:

1	fresh baguette, cut into 24 slices about 1/4 to 1/2 inch (0.5 to 1 cm) thick, with about 4 inches (10 cm) on either end reserved for the aioli	1
4 tbsp	olive oil	60 ml
	Canola oil (for frying)	
24	fresh oysters, shucked and drained	24
1 cup	bread crumbs	250 ml
1	small red onion, cut into very thin slices	1
6	cherry tomatoes	6

1 Remove the crusts from the baguette ends and tear the remaining white bread into chunks. Soak the bread with the milk in a small bowl for 10 minutes or so. Remove the bread and squeeze it tightly in your hands so that you get all the milk out.

2 Toss the bread and the garlic cloves into your food processor and run it, turning on and off in pulses, until you get a nice paste consistency.

3 Turn the processor on and add the egg yolks through the spout. Once the yolks have mixed (it should only take a few seconds), pour the olive oil in a thin stream until you get a nice thick and creamy aioli.

4 Transfer the mixture to a bowl and stir in the lemon juice, chives, Tabasco, salt, and fresh cracked pepper. Refrigerate immediately until ready to use.

5 Preheat your oven to 350°F (180°C). Brush one side of the baguette slices with the olive oil and place them oiled-side-up on a baking sheet. Bake in the oven until toasty brown. Remove from the oven to cool.

6 Fill a large high-sided skillet with canola oil until you get a

2-inch (5-cm) depth and heat over a high heat until your candy thermometer reads 375°F (190°C).

7 Dredge the oysters in the bread crumbs and fry in the oil, 4 or 5 at a time until golden brown, about 1 minute. Transfer the oysters to a bowl lined with paper towels.

8 To serve, place a slice of the red onion on each of the baguette slices and top with a dollop of the aioli. Put 4 of the slices on each of the serving plate around 1 of the cherry tomatoes. Place 1 of the crispy hot oysters on each of the baguette slices and serve immediately.

Bar-b-qued Oysters with Tequila Lime Butter

40	large Canadian oysters, unopened and scrubbed clean	40
1 cup	unsalted butter	250 ml
	Juice of 1 lime	
	Grated peel of the same lime	
1 tbsp	tequila (preferably Gold tequila)	15 ml
	Salt and freshly cracked pepper, to taste	
36	Melba toast rounds	36

1 Preheat your bar-b-que to medium-high or set your oven on broil.

2 Place the oysters on the grill or under the broiler and cook for 5 to 8 minutes until the shells open, turning them once or twice. Discard any that fail to open after 8 minutes.

3 Meanwhile, melt the butter in a small saucepan over a medium heat. Add the lime juice, lime peel, and tequila and mix well. Add salt and freshly cracked pepper to taste.

4 Place 6 oysters on each serving plate, alternating with a Melba toast round standing vertically on its end. Using a teaspoon, drizzle the butter over the oysters and serve immediately.

Some of the best oyster months typically see most of Canada buried under a mountain of snow, so you can also do this one in the oven under the broiler. Try it as a starter to Christmas dinner or on any cold wintery night and wash them down with sangria! You can also leave the tequila out without any other adjustment if you are so inclined. We suggest 40 oysters in case some don't open; everyone will still get a six-pack. The Melba toast is a nice crunchy counterpoint to the slurpy goodness of the warm salty-tartness of the grilled oysters.

Serves 6 as an appetizer

The Astorville Parish Picnic

21

For the last 70-odd years, the good people of Astorville in northern Ontario have held their parish picnic on the second Sunday in August. Astorville is fairly representative of your average small Canadian town where French and British traditions live happily side by side. The picnic indulges the English passion of a fine pipe band (C4 Highlanders front and present!), and *l'influence franco* is most obvious in the communal late afternoon meal featuring hearty plate loads of succulent cipaille.

Cipaille, fellow foodies, is unlike anything you've ever had before. It is best enjoyed on a paper plate served up with a heaping side of slaw, potato salad, and fresh tomato-cucumber salad and eaten at a long communal table. Preparing this dish is a community event and many a small town from the Maritimes to the

Prairies lay claim to the definitive recipe. As there are regional variations for risotto in Italy, so goes it for cipaille in Canada. It is a giant stew-like layered affair requiring hundreds of pounds of beef, chicken, pork, potatoes, onions, and spices separated by several layers of delicious homemade dough and baked in blackened 18-inch (45-cm) cauldrons until the top layer of crust is a bubbly golden brown. The satisfaction is as much in the making as in the eating. Picture dozens of folks sitting around peeling, laughing, crying (from the onions), making dough, and gossiping, the flour flying, kids yelling, coffee brewing, and smiles galore. Each cauldron requires some 25 pounds (12.5 kg) of meat and such to conjure a delectable cipaille. Dinner is served in the parish hall with all the side dishes and condiments you would expect at a proper country picnic.

A detail of men stay up the night before tending to huge outdoor ovens, until cord after cord of wood has been reduced to ash, leaving the brick oven walls white-hot and ready for their charges. Only then are the cauldrons (each requiring two people to carry it) inserted therein for a slow bake. Hours later, the heady aromas from these percolating pies overwhelm all in attendance. The ovens are then ceremoniously opened and the cipaille are loaded into the back of flatbed pick-up trucks for a slow, careful drive over to the parish hall. Word of their pending arrival reaches the waiting citizenry in advance of the convoy, as tummies rumble in anticipation of this once-a-year treat.

All food tastes better when prepared and consumed with friends and family. If you can't get to Astorville next August, check out a community picnic or potluck dinner in your home town. Chances are you'll experience the same warmth and sharing, which, after all, is the secret ingredient common to all memorable meals.

Here then are three wonderful one-pot dinners, plus some side dishes, in honour of our friends in Astorville.

Creamy Cold Cucumber and Bell Pepper Soup

2	medium cucumbers, peeled, seeded, and coarsely chopped	2
2	medium yellow bell peppers, seeded and coarsely chopped	2
2 cups	diced honeydew melon	500 ml
2	shallots, finely diced	2
1/2 cup	plain yoghurt	125 ml
	Juice of 1/2 lemon	
	Juice of 1 lime	
	Salt and freshly cracked pepper	
1	bunch basil, washed, stems removed, and torn by hand	1
	Chives, coarsely chopped (for garnish)	

This is a great chilled soup for a warm summer day. Use a teaspoon to seed the cucumbers.

Serves 6

1 Combine all the ingredients, except for the basil and chives, in a blender or food processor and purée. Strain through a fine sieve into a large bowl. Stir in the basil and chill for at least 2 hours.

2 Serve the soup with a sprinkle of chives and some crunchy croutons.

Chicken and Veggie Salad with Lemon Vinaigrette

This is an easy summer picnic recipe that is a snap to put together at the last minute. The only real prep work is in cooking the chicken and sweet potatoes. If you're going to transport the salad to a picnic site, keep the salad dressing, feta cheese, and basil leaves separate until you're ready to toss and serve to avoid sogginess.

Serves 6 with lots left over

3	carrots, peeled and coarsely chopped into bite-size pieces	3
2	bunches broccoli, florets cut from stems and separated	2
18	snow peas, trimmed	18
6	half chicken breasts, skin removed and grilled or baked	6
2	medium sweet potatoes, peeled and sliced into 1/2-inch (1-cm) medallions, then grilled or baked	2
1	12 oz/350 ml can water chestnuts, drained and halved	1
1/2	red bell pepper, diced	1/2
1/2	yellow bell pepper, diced	1/2
	Salt and freshly cracked pepper	
1/2 cup	olive oil	125 ml
	Juice of 1 lemon	
1 tsp	dried thyme	5 ml
3/4 lb	feta cheese	350 g
1	small red onion, halved and thinly sliced	1
20	basil leaves, stems removed and hand-torn in half	20

1 Steam the carrots and broccoli over a pot of boiling water for 3 minutes or until just tender but still crispy. Add the snow peas and steam for 30 seconds longer. Transfer the veggies to a large bowl to cool.

2 Cut the chicken into bite-size chunks and halve the sweet potato medallions so they look like half moons. If you've grilled them, you'll have those wonderful grill marks everywhere. Add the chicken and sweet potato to the cooled veggies. Throw in the water chestnuts and the bell peppers. Season to taste with salt and freshly cracked pepper.

3 Mix the olive oil, lemon juice, and thyme in a bowl and whisk to make the dressing. Season with salt and freshly cracked pepper. Pour the dressing over the salad and add the feta, red onion, and basil leaves. Toss well and serve.

Curried Lamb and Sweet Potato Stew

4 lbs	lamb stewing meat, trimmed and cut into bite-size chunks	2 kg
	Salt and freshly cracked pepper	
4 tbsp	all-purpose flour (for dredging)	60 ml
4 tbsp	olive oil	60 ml
4	garlic cloves, minced	4
2 tbsp	curry powder	30 ml
1 cup	red wine	250 ml
1 quart	water	1 L
2	cinnamon sticks	2
2 1/2 lbs	sweet potatoes, peeled and cut into bite-size chunks	1 kg
1	large can (28 oz/796 ml) baked beans	1

We purposely made this recipe for eight instead of the usual six because this is one you'll want to have as leftovers. If you're not a lamb aficionado, then you can easily substitute the same quantity of beef or pork tenderloin. You can also adjust the amount of curry powder depending on your SFT (Spicy Food Threshold).

Serves 8

1 Season the lamb with salt and fresh cracked pepper. Lightly dredge the lamb chunks in the flour.
2 Heat the oil in a large pot over a medium-high heat and add the garlic and curry powder. Sauté for 1 minute.
3 Add the lamb chunks and continue to cook. Stirring often, sauté the lamb until browned on all sides, about 10 minutes.
4 Add the wine and cook for another 4 minutes.
5 Add the water, cinnamon sticks, and sweet potatoes. Mix well and simmer uncovered for 45 minutes until the lamb is cooked through and the liquid has reduced to a thick sauce consistency.
6 Add the beans and continue to cook for another 4 minutes.
7 Serve in big bowls with lots of warm crusty bread and unsalted butter.

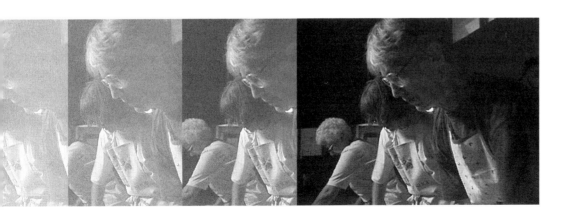

Cipaille

Like pasta and pizza in Italy, this dish has many regional variations from one French-Canadian community to another. It is generally accepted that cipaille is Acadian in origin. When we travelled to Astorville we found that it was a once-a-year dish that took most of the community to make. Their version comes in huge cast-iron cauldrons, baked overnight in huge brick ovens for consumption the next day by the entire parish. Yummers. Here is a scaled-down recipe perfect for you to try at home. Don't forget that you have to start this one the night before cooking.

Serves 8 as a main course with leftovers

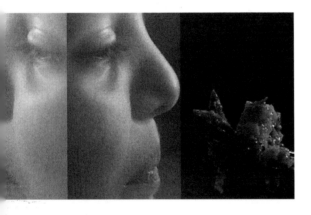

2 lbs	boneless chicken breasts	1 kg
2 lbs	lean stewing beef	1 kg
2 lbs	pork shoulder roast	1 kg
3	large cooking onions, chopped	3
6	celery stalks, chopped	6
6	garlic cloves, diced	6
1 tsp	salt	5 ml
1 tsp	freshly ground pepper	5 ml
1 tsp	dried sage	5 ml
1 tsp	dried thyme	5 ml
1	3-in/7.5-cm cinnamon stick	1
1/2 tsp	nutmeg	2 ml
1/4 lb	salt pork, diced	115 g
2 cups	peeled and cubed potatoes	500 ml
9 in	double crust pastry dough	23 cm
1 1/2 cups	chicken stock	375 ml
1 1/2 cups	beef stock	375 ml

1 Cut the chicken, beef, and pork into 1-in (2.5-cm) chunks. Place them in a large non-reactive bowl with the onion, celery, and garlic.
2 Add the salt, pepper, sage, thyme, cinnamon, and nutmeg. Mix well, cover, and refrigerate overnight.
3 Preheat your oven to 400°F (200°C).
4 Get out a large 3-quart (3-L) casserole dish (preferably cast-iron) and arrange the salt pork on the bottom.
5 Layer ⅓ of the meat mixture and ⅓ of the potatoes onto the salt pork.
6 Roll out ⅓ of the pastry dough and place on top of the meat and potato mixture, cutting a little hole in the centre of the dough.
7 Repeat the process twice more till you have a nicely layered cipaille, finishing with the last of the pastry dough (don't forget the hole in the middle).
8 Slowly pour the 2 stocks through the hole in the pastry till liquid appears.
9 Cover the cipaille and bake in the middle of the oven for about 1 hour, or until the liquid simmers.
10 Reduce heat to 250°F (120°C) and continue to bake for another 5.5 hours.

Buttermilk Slaw

1	large green cabbage, cut in half with the tough outer leaves removed	1
1/2	small red cabbage, tough outer leaves removed	1/2
1	large carrot, peeled and julienned or grated	1
1/2	small red onion, finely diced	1/2
1/2 cup	raisins or dried currants	125 ml
2 tbsp	minced fresh chives	30 ml
2/3 cup	cold buttermilk	150 ml
1/2 cup	mayonnaise	125 ml
1 tsp	mustard (Dijon or sweet honey mustard would be nice)	5 ml
1 tsp	sugar	5 ml
	Salt and freshly cracked pepper	

Here's a nice change from the same-ol' same-ol' slaw. It's great on picnics or as part of a light summer meal. Once upon a time, buttermilk was the liquid left over after churning, but these days it's made commercially. It has a thick texture and a slight tang to it that adds a pleasantly different zing to the slaw. If you like, throw in a handful of toasted pine nuts or sunflower seeds for a crunchy bite to your salad.

Serves 6 as a side dish

1 Place each of the cabbage halves flat-side-down on a cutting board and slice into thin strips.
2 Toss the cabbage slices, carrot, onion, and raisins in a large bowl.
3 Whisk the remaining ingredients together and pour over the cabbage mixture. Toss again and season with salt and fresh cracked pepper.

Three Bean Salad with Veggies

This is a very nice change from the standard picnic potato salad. It travels very well and takes practically no time at all to whip up.

Serves 6 as a side dish

3/4 lb	green beans	350 g
2/3 cup	olive oil	150 ml
	Juice of 1 lemon	
1/2	bunch chives, coarsely diced	1/2
	Salt and freshly cracked pepper, to taste	
1 cup	canned black beans, rinsed and picked over	250 ml
1 cup	canned white beans (such as pinto beans or chickpeas), rinsed and picked over	250 ml
3	plum tomatoes, halved, seeded, and coarsely chopped	3
3	celery stalks, coarsely chopped	3
2	carrots, peeled and finely diced	2
3	radishes, washed and thinly sliced (optional)	3

1 Bring a large pot of salted water to boil over high heat and add the green beans. Cook them for about 4 minutes or until al dente. Drain and let cool.
2 Combine the olive oil, lemon juice, chives, salt, and fresh cracked pepper in a large bowl and whisk. Add the beans, tomatoes, celery, carrots, and radishes. Snap the green beans in half using your hands. . . . feel the green bean . . . why use an impersonal knife when you can feel your food . . . once snapped, add those yummy green beans to the mixture and stir thoroughly. Season to taste with salt and fresh cracked pepper.

Recipes from the Columns

22

If you are a regular *Great Canadian Food Show* viewer, then you know that our "Cooking with Spirits" and "Kitchen Jim" columns have some of the best recipes on the show. We've received thousands of letters requesting these dishes. Here are some of the best from the columns.

Shrimp Flambé with Proscuitto

When *The Great Canadian Food Show* first went to air, the *Ottawa Citizen* did a very generous story on us in their food section. We offered this recipe to the paper's readers as part of that story and, at the end of the year, *Ottawa Citizen* readers voted it one of the 10 best recipes of the year. This one is quite simple, yet dramatic in its preparation. Flambéing simply means to ignite a spirit and allow its alcohol content to burn off, thus concentrating the flavourful essence and eliminating the harsh edge of the alcohol. Cooking with wine, spirits, and beer is an easy way to bring incredible new tastes to your meals.

In this dish, the plump, meaty shrimp serve as a culinary canvas for the interesting play between the saltiness of the proscuitto and the sweetness of the Grand Marnier. When flambéed, the proscuitto wrap turns an amazing burnt-orange colour. Serve the shrimp set upon two heaping spoonfuls of risotto, on a toasted baguette slice, or with sliced honeydew melon. Try ouzo, brandy, or tequila as variations on the theme.

Serves 6 as an appetizer

12	jumbo shrimp, peeled and deveined	12
12	slices of good-quality proscuitto (cut that day from the haunch and not vacuum-packed; no other ham will do as a substitute)	12
2 tbsp	unsalted butter	30 ml
6	large shallots, finely diced	6
1 cup	Grand Marnier	250 ml

1 Wrap each shrimp in a slice of proscuitto (the ham is oily enough to hold it together).
2 In a large frying pan melt half the butter over medium heat. Add half the shallots and sauté for about 3 minutes or until the shallots are tender.
3 Add 6 of the shrimp to the pan and sauté for about 30 seconds per side or until the proscuitto turns a burnt-orange colour.
4 Add half the Grand Marnier and swirl around the pan. Remove the pan from the heat and tilt away from you. Light the liqueur with a match. Remember that you're lighting the fumes, so the match doesn't have to go right into the liquid. And don't worry about burning your eyebrows off, as the flame will subside almost immediately as the airborne vapours are instantly burned away.
5 Return the pan to the heat and allow the flame to die out naturally. If you try to put the flame out yourself by putting a lid on the pan, you will leave an acrid alcohol taste in the ruined dish. Blah.
6 Once the flame is out and the liquid has been reduced to a syrupy consistency, pour the shrimp and the Grand Marnier syrup into a bowl and tent with foil to keep warm; repeat with the remaining shrimp.

Curried Squash Soup

3 1/2 lbs	butternut or acorn squash	1.5 kg
3 tbsp	olive oil	45 ml
2 tbsp	unsalted butter	30 ml
1	large onion, diced	1
2	carrots, peeled and diced	2
3	garlic cloves, diced	3
1 tbsp	curry powder	15 ml
1 1/2 quarts	chicken stock	1.5 L
1 cup	35% cream	250 ml
	Chives, coarsely chopped (for garnish)	
	Salt and freshly cracked pepper	

You're going to love this soup. The curry really sets the roasted squash off nicely. Resist adding more curry than we call for, even if you love dishes spicy, otherwise you'll mask the sweet roasted taste of the squash.

Serves 6 as a starter

1 Preheat oven to 350°F (180°C). Slice the squash in half. Pour the olive oil on your hands and rub the cut faces of the squash. Place the squash cut-side-down on a baking sheet and roast in the middle of the oven for about 40 minutes or until cooked through.

2 Melt the butter in a soup pot over medium-high heat and add the onion and carrots. Sauté for 4 minutes. Reduce the heat to medium and add the garlic and curry powder. Sauté for 2 minutes. The butter will act on the curry powder and garlic. Combined with the onion, it will fill your kitchen with an incredible aroma that will set everybody salivating.

3 Using a big spoon, scoop the squash out of its skin and into the soup pot. Chuck the skin. Pour in the chicken stock and stir to mix well. Increase the heat to medium-high and bring to a gentle boil. Cover the pot and simmer for 20 minutes so that all of the flavours blend nicely.

4 Remove the soup pot from the heat and purée, either in a blender or using a hand mixer. At this point you can let the soup sit until you're ready to serve. When ready to eat, pour in the cream, mix well, and reheat over low heat, stirring occasionally. Do not let the soup boil! Season to taste with salt and pepper. Divide the soup among the serving bowls and sprinkle with chives. Serve immediately.

Pan-Seared Breast of Duck in Soy-Honey Sauce

This recipe is a variation on one I first had in the small town of Sisteron in the south of France (how's that for pretentious?). The chef refused to give me his secret recipe, so I spent the rest of my honeymoon reverse-engineering the recipe until I got it right. The fresh rosemary is an addition that heightens the complexity of tastes. This is possibly the easiest special-occasion main course there is, and it proves the maxim that a few simple fresh ingredients can make something wondrous. Make this once and I guarantee it becomes a keeper.

Serves 6 as a main course

2	duck breasts (each about 1 lb/450 g)	2
	Salt and freshly cracked pepper	
2 tbsp	finely diced fresh rosemary	30 ml
2/3 cup	liquid honey	150 ml
1/2 cup	good-quality soy sauce	125 ml
3 tbsp	maple syrup	45 ml
6 tbsp	fresh rosemary, removed from the stem but not chopped	90 ml
	Fresh berries in season (preferably raspberries but must be a red meat berry) or dried cranberries (for garnish)	

1 Preheat your oven to 350°F (180°C).
2 Pat the duck breasts dry and sprinkle with salt, fresh cracked pepper, and the chopped rosemary.
3 In a medium pan, fry the duck fat-side-down over a medium heat. When the fat begins to melt, increase the heat to medium-high and continue to cook for another 4 minutes or until the fat is crispy brown on the outside. Turn the duck over and continue to cook for another 4 minutes.
4 Remove duck breasts from pan, tent with foil, and put in the oven to finish. After 5 minutes, turn the oven off, leaving the duck breasts inside to remain warm.
5 Meanwhile add honey, soy sauce, and maple syrup to the same pan and bring to a quick boil. Immediately reduce heat, add unchopped rosemary, and scrape up any juicy delicious brown bits clinging to the bottom of the pan. Simmer 1 or 2 minutes longer.
6 Remove duck from oven and let sit for 5 minutes so that internal juices settle.
7 While the duck is resting, strain the sauce through a fine sieve and cover the bottom of each serving plate with the strained sauce.
8 Cut the duck breasts into thin slices against the grain. Arrange the slices into a decorative teepee on each plate.
9 Arrange a few of the berries on each plate. Serve with roasted potatoes or risotto plated at the centre of the teepee. Sit back and wait for the applause.

Cedar-Plank Salmon Marinated in Brandy and Earl Grey Tea

6	cedar shingles (available at hardware or lumber stores)	6
3/4 cup	good-quality brandy	175 ml
6 tbsp	maple syrup	90 ml
3 tbsp	soy sauce	45 ml
4	Earl Grey tea bags	4
2 tsp	uncracked black peppercorns	10 ml
2	garlic cloves, crushed	2
6	salmon fillets, skin on	6

1 Soak the cedar shingles in a tub of water for at least 1 hour and up to 3 hours. Use some sort of waterproof weight to keep them all submerged.

2 Combine all the ingredients in a non-reactive casserole dish and add the salmon fillets, turning them often to ensure they are well covered. Marinate skin-side-down at room temperature for 30 minutes.

3 Remove oven rack and preheat your oven to 450°F (230°C).

4 Place the cedar shingles on the oven rack. Place 1 salmon fillet skin-side-down on each shingle.

5 Return oven rack to centre of the oven and bake the salmon for 10 minutes.

6 Plate the salmon on or off the cedar shingle and serve with rice or roasted potatoes and colourful veggies, such as a red pepper–carrot–asparagus medley.

This recipe is a variation on one first introduced to us by Chef Judd Simpson, who holds court over the kitchens of Parliament Hill in Ottawa. Judd is one of a new breed of young chefs who are constantly on the lookout for innovative ways of preparing fresh seasonal ingredients. The cedar plank imparts a wonderful orange hue to the salmon when baked at a high heat.

Serves 6 as a main course

Chicken in Whisky Peanut Sauce

The episode we did about Vancouver's Chinatown (see Chapter 5) set out to celebrate the variety of pan-Asian influences now available in most Canadian communities. In this recipe we decided to return the favour and modify a classic Asian peanut sauce by including a decidedly Canadian ingredient...whisky. As with all of our recipes that involve spirits, the alcohol content is boiled away in the cooking process, leaving only the rich, complex whisky tastes that come from the aging process. Best of all, this is another one-pan meal, so there is minimum clean-up time. We like to use three times the garlic we suggest in the recipe because we're garlic-crazy. You can also add dried chili pepper.

Serves 6 as a main course

6	boneless half chicken breasts, trimmed of fat and skin removed	6
	Salt and freshly cracked pepper	
4 tbsp	unsalted butter	60 ml
1/2 lb	unsalted dry-roasted peanuts	225 g
1	medium onion, diced	1
3 tbsp	diced fresh ginger	45 ml
3 tbsp	diced garlic	45 ml
1	red pepper, halved and cored, then sliced into long thin strips	1
1	green pepper, halved and cored, then sliced into long thin strips	1
1 cup	smooth peanut butter	250 ml
4 tbsp	soy sauce	60 ml
2/3 cup	Canadian whisky	150 ml
1 1/2 cups	chicken stock	375 ml

1 Pat the chicken breasts dry and season with salt and fresh cracked pepper.
2 Melt half the butter in a large skillet over a medium-high heat. Cook the chicken breasts, 3 at time, in the butter for 3 minutes per side or until a nice crispy brown exterior develops, turning only once. Add more butter between the two batches of chicken breasts, if necessary.
3 Put the chicken aside on a plate and tent with tin foil.
4 Add remaining butter and dry-roasted peanuts. Sauté for 1 minute.
5 Add onion and ginger and sauté for 5 minutes. Add garlic and sauté for an additional 30 seconds.
6 Add the red and green peppers and continue to sauté for 1 minute.
7 Add peanut butter and soy sauce. Mix until a thick sauce consistency is reached.
8 Add whisky and stock, stir, and bring to a boil. Reduce heat and simmer for 7 minutes. Return chicken to the pan and continue to simmer until chicken is heated through and sauce has reduced a bit, about 7 minutes longer.
9 Serve the chicken on a bed of basmati rice with grilled asparagus or sweet baby peas.

The Martooni Salad

1/2 cup	gin	125 ml
1 cup	walnut oil	250 ml
Splash	dry vermouth	Splash
	Mesclun (enough for 6 small servings)	
3	shallots, diced	3
12	large pimento-stuffed olives	12

1 Whisk the gin, oil, and vermouth together and toss with the mesclun and shallots in a large bowl.
2 Place one-sixth of the greens in each martini glass.
3 Skewer 2 olives on a toothpick and place on top of the salad. Repeat with the other glasses.

This is a fun and super-simple salad for an adult dinner party. The gin gives the dressing a lovely juniper berry taste. Get yourself some honkin'-big martini glasses to serve the salad in. Any number of spirits can easily be substituted for vinegar in your salad dressing. Go crazy and experiment with dark Jamaican rum, tequila, or Frangelico.

Serves 6 as a starter salad

Strawberries in Red Wine with Fresh Cracked Pepper

1	28-oz/750-ml bottle of good red wine (such as a VQA Cabernet Sauvignon)	1
4 tbsp	freshly cracked black pepper	60 ml
1 cup	sugar	250 ml
3 pints	fresh strawberries, washed and hulled	1.5 L

1 In a small saucepan, bring red wine to a boil. Reduce heat to medium and simmer until the wine has reduced by half.
2 Add cracked black pepper and sugar. Stir until the sugar has completely dissolved. Remove from heat and let sit at room temperature for at least 1 hour.
3 Put the strawberries in a large non-reactive bowl and strain the wine reduction through a fine sieve lined with a coffee filter over the berries.
4 Let the berries marinate for at least 1 hour and serve with fresh whipped cream.

There are only four ingredients in this easy dessert recipe, so don't skimp on the quality of the red wine you use! This obviously is a summer recipe, as fresh strawberries are a must. It still amazes us that folks will pay an arm and a leg for the pale cardboard berries we get from faraway greenhouses in the off season. Remember: Buy fresh, buy local, buy Canadian!

Serves 6 as a dessert

Peaches with Brandy

In the entire universe of food, there are only a few occasions where we would ever consider using a canned or bottled product over a fresh one. The most obvious occasions are when the product has been altered, such as stewed tomatoes or anchovies or brined olives. You gotta be crazy to go to the huge amount of trouble required to brine your own fresh olives. For this dessert, we acknowledge that peeling and pitting your own peach halves is a giant pain in the wazoo and suggest that canned clingstone peaches are okay as a substitute unless you've got way too much free time and no hobbies.

This is a very easy dessert to prepare. You can experiment by substituting Armagnac, grappa, Grand Marnier, or malt whisky for the brandy in exactly the same quantity.

Serves 6 as a dessert

1/3 cup	unsalted butter	75 ml
1 cup	sugar	250 ml
1 1/2 cups	brandy	375 ml
Pinch	cinnamon	Pinch
12	peach halves, peeled and pitted	12

1 Preheat your oven to 350°F (180°C).
2 In a medium saucepan, combine all of the ingredients, except for the peaches, and warm over medium-low heat until the sugar has completely dissolved. Be careful not to boil, as you don't want the alcohol to burn away until in the oven.
3 Place peach halves cut-side-down on a baking pan. Pour the brandy mixture over the peach halves and bake in the middle of the oven for about 30 minutes, basting occasionally.
4 Serve 2 peach halves per person over good vanilla ice cream. Drizzle with the remaining brandy liquid, which should be a yummy syrupy texture by now. Stick a cinnamon stick and a fresh mint sprig into the ice cream as garnish.

Index

Aceto Balsamico vinegar, 66–67
Aioli and Chives, Skinny Oyster
    Po-Boy with, 130–131
Anjou pear, 84
apple wine, 85
apples
    Apples with Cinnamon Calvados
        Cream, 14
    Roasted Apple Coulis,
        Cherrywood-Grilled Arctic Char
        with, 121
asparagus
    Asparagus Soup with Chive Oil, 28
    Grilled Asparagus and Pork
        Salad, 4
    Pork and Asparagus-Stuffed
        Parmesan Baskets, 109
Astorville (Ontario), 132–133
Au'Coin, Claude, 56–57

Baby Spinach and Mushroom Salad
    with Gorgonzola Cheese and
    Pears Poached in Strawberry
    Wine with Orange Vinaigrette,
    84–85
Ballentine, George, 26
Balsamic Rhubarb Compote, 67
Bar-b-qued Moose, 61
Bar-b-qued Oysters with Tequila
    Lime Butter, 131
Bar-b-qued Pineapple, 7
Bar-b-qued Sardines, 5
bar-b-ques, 1–2
    Bar-b-qued Moose, 61
    Bar-b-qued Oysters with Tequila
        Lime Butter, 131
    Bar-b-qued Pineapple, 7
    Bar-b-qued Sardines, 5
    Grilled Asparagus and Pork
        Salad, 4
    Grilled Leg of Lamb, 3
    Grilled Scallops with Sun-Dried
        Tomato Sauce, 58
    Grilled Sea Bass with Watermelon-
        Mango Salsa, 24
    Lemon Grilled Zucchini, 6
    Roasted Apple Coulis,
        Cherrywood-Grilled Arctic Char
        with, 121
    tips for, 3
The Basic Bird, 39–40
beans. See legumes
Beaver Club, 90

beef. See meats
Beef and Pork Stew, 114–115
Beet Emulsions, Chicken Ballentine
    with Carrot Butter and, 26–27
Bell Pepper Soup, Creamy Cold
    Cucumber and, 133
Bernardo, Adolpho, 12
Bernardo, Mario, 12
berry wine, 83
The Best Ever Meat Loaf, 46
blueberries
    Blueberry Poivrade (Roast Loin of
        Caribou Lac St. Jean with
        Smoked Corn and Buckwheat
        Croquette and Berry Chutney
        in), 92–94
    Blueberry Sauce, 88–89
    blueberry wine, 88
    *Sassie de Caribou aux Petits Fruits
        des Marais*, 15–16
Bobby Burns Lodge, 1
Bocuse, Paul, 90
Boisvert, Katherine, 124
bouillabaisse, 12–13
Boulay, Jean-Luc, 15
Braised Short Ribs with Roasted Red
    Pepper and Red Wine Sauce,
    102–103
braising, 53, 102
breads, 72
Buckwheat Croquette (and Berry
    Chutney in Blueberry Poivrade,
    Roast Loin of Caribou Lac St. Jean
    with Smoked Corn and), 92–94
Buffalo Eggplant Stew, 65
Bugaboo Couscous, 6
Bulgur Wheat and Wild Rice Risotto
    with Woodland Mushrooms,
    97–98
Burleigh Brothers, 25
butter
    Basil Balsamic Butter, Corn and
        Tomatoes in, 71
    Carrot Butter and Beet Emulsions,
        Chicken Ballentine with, 26–27
    clarified, 29
    Frangelico Butter Sauce,
        Homemade Ravioli Stuffed with
        Roasted Squash and Goat Cheese
        in, 74–75
    Pear Wine Butter Sauce, 87–88
    Porcini Butter, Chicken Breasts
        Stuffed with Wild Mushrooms
        and, 50–51

    Tequila Lime Butter, Bar-b-qued
        Oysters with, 131
Buttermilk Slaw, 137

Cabbage Bean Soup, 46–47
Le Café Monde, 9–11
cakes. See dessert
Calf's Liver with Bacon, Herbs, and
    Balsamic Vinegar, 70–71
Canadian Cuisine, 59
Canadian Mountain Holidays, 1–2
Canadian wine, 101–102
Caramelized Peaches, 100
caribou. See meats
carrots
    Carrot Butter and Beet Emulsions,
        Chicken Ballentine with, 26–27
    Honey-Buttered Carrots, Steak
        and Frites with, 111
Cassis Sauce, Pork Tenderloin in a,
    113
Cedar-Plank Salmon Marinated in
    Brandy and Earl Grey Tea, 143
Chateau Halifax, 83
Chateau Whistler, 108
cheese
    Baby Spinach and Mushroom Salad
        with Gorgonzola Cheese and
        Pears Poached in Strawberry
        Wine with Orange Vinaigrette,
        84–85
    *Frivolité de Saumon Fumée au
        Poireau et Fromage de Chèvre*, 17
    Gnocchi alla Gorgonzola, 73
    goat, 52
    Grilled Breast of Chicken Filled
        with Oka Cheese and Fresh Sage,
        96–97
    Homemade Ravioli Stuffed with
        Roasted Squash and Goat Cheese
        in Frangelico Butter Sauce, 74–75
    New Potato, Goat Cheese, and
        Green Bean Salad with Sweet
        Balsamic Vinaigrette, 68
    Wild Mushroom and Goat Cheese
        Omelette, 52–53
cheesecloth, 32
Chernoff, Eleanor, 46
Cherrywood-Grilled Arctic Char
    with Roasted Apple Coulis, 121
chicken. See poultry
Chicken and Veggie Salad with
    Lemon Vinaigrette, 134

Chicken Ballentine with Carrot
    Butter and Beet Emulsions,
    26–27
Chicken Breasts in Riesling Sauce,
    105
Chicken Breasts Stuffed with Wild
    Mushrooms and Porcini Butter,
    50–51
Chicken in Whisky Peanut Sauce,
    144
Chilled Smoked Salmon Soup with
    Chive Oil, 110–111
Chinatown, 30–37
Chinese five spice powder, 34
Chive Oil, Chilled Smoked Salmon
    Soup with, 110–111
Chocolate and Roasted Walnut Tart
    with Caramelized Peaches and
    Raspberry Sorbet, 100
Cinnamon Calvados Cream, Apples
    with, 14
Cinnamon Crust Breast of Turkey
    with Sweet and Spicy Thai Cream
    Sauce, 60–61
Cipaille, 132–133, 136
Clams, Tomatoes, and Arugula,
    Linguine with, 78
Clark, Rodney, 127–128
coconut milk, 123
Coconut Soup (Tom Kha Gai), Thai
    Spicy, 32
Cold Shrimp and Noodle Salad, 37
columns, 139
Compote, Balsamic Rhubarb, 67
Confit de Canard, Pommes à l'Ail, 11
"Cooking with Spirits," 139
Cordeau, Jean, 90
Corn and Tomatoes in Basil Balsamic
    Butter, 71
cottage cheese filling, for perogies,
    45
Couscous, Bugaboo, 6
Crab Shack, 128
Craig, David, 18
Cranberry Cream Sauce, Venison
    Shoulder Roast with, 62
Creamy Cold Cucumber and Bell
    Pepper Soup, 133
Culinary Grand Prix, 108
Curried Lamb and Sweet Potato
    Stew, 135
Curried Squash Soup, 141
Czapalay, Sharlene, 25
Czapalay, Stefan, 25

dessert
  Apples with Cinnamon Calvados
    Cream, 14
  Chocolate and Roasted Walnut Tart
    with Caramelized Peaches and
    Raspberry Sorbet, 100
  Five-Minute Fudge, 47
  Key Lime Cheesecake Boisvert,
    124–125
  Peaches with Brandy, 146
  Pecan Pumpkin Torte, 125–126
  Poppy Seed Cake, 48
  Strawberries in Red Wine with
    Fresh Cracked Pepper, 145
Digby (Nova Scotia), 56
Digby Scallop Mousse, 57
Digby sea scallop, 55–57
Dim Sum Shrimp Dumplings with
  Three Dipping Sauces, 34–35
dressings
  Lemon Vinaigrette, Chicken and
    Veggie Salad with, 134
  Orange Vinaigrette, Baby Spinach
    and Mushroom Salad with
    Gorgonzola Cheese and Pears
    Poached in Strawberry Wine
    with, 84–85
  Sweet Balsamic Vinaigrette, New
    Potato, Goat Cheese, and Green
    Bean Salad with, 68
dry scallop, 56
duck. See poultry
Duck Mountain Motel, 43

Eggplant Stew, Buffalo, 65
eggs
  raw yolks, 10
  Stefan's Mushroom Flan, 29
  Wild Mushroom and Goat Cheese
    Omelette, 52–53
Elizabeth, Queen, 95–96

The Fabled Maritime Lobster Roll, 82
Field, Chris, 127–128
Fillet of Atlantic Halibut Poached in
  Telderberry Pear Wine with Pear
  Wine Butter Sauce, 87–88
fish and shellfish
  Bar-b-qued Oysters with Tequila
    Lime Butter, 131
  Bar-b-qued Sardines, 5
  Cedar-Plank Salmon Marinated in
    Brandy and Earl Grey Tea, 143
  Cherrywood-Grilled Arctic Char
    with Roasted Apple Coulis, 121
  Chilled Smoked Salmon Soup with
    Chive Oil, 110–111
  Cold Shrimp and Noodle Salad, 37

Digby Scallop Mousse, 57
Digby sea scallop, 55–57
Dim Sum Shrimp Dumplings with
  Three Dipping Sauces, 34–35
dry scallop, 56
The Fabled Maritime Lobster
  Roll, 82
Fillet of Atlantic Halibut Poached
  in Telderberry Pear Wine with
  Pear Wine Butter Sauce, 87–88
Frivolité de Saumon Fumée au
  Poireau et Fromage de Chèvre, 17
Grilled Scallops with Sun-Dried
  Tomato Sauce, 58
Grilled Sea Bass with Watermelon-
  Mango Salsa, 24
Leek and Mussel Soup, 117–118
Linguine with Clams, Tomatoes,
  and Arugula, 78
lobster, 80
Maritime Oyster Chowder with
  Telderberry Apple Wine and
  Sweet Curried Whipped Cream,
  85–86
Most Excellent Fish Soup, 12–13
Mussels in Coconut and Lime
  Nectar, 123
The Nutty Trout, 22–23
oyster shucking, 127–128
oysters, 25–26, 85
Pan-Fried Oysters with Spicy
  Salsa, 129
patting dry, 105
P.E.I. Mussels with Cherry
  Tomatoes, Herbs and Cream, 118
raw fish, 10
Roasted Lobster with Lemon Chive
  Oil, 81
Shrimp Flambé with Proscuitto, 140
Skinny Oyster Po-Boy with Aioli
  and Chives, 130–131
Smoked Salmon and Arctic Char
  Tartare with Herb Sauce, 91
Super-Fast Mussels with Garlic
  and Herbs, 122
Tartare aux Deux Saumons, 10
Truite en Colère avec Sauce Beurre
  Blanc, 20–22
Vietnamese Beef and Shrimp
  Noodle Soup, 33
fish sauce, 33, 37
Five-Minute Fudge, 47
five spice powder, 34
flambéing, 140
Flank Steak, Marinated Asian, 36–37
Foie Gras à l'Armagnac, 16
foil, 103
Foster, Jim, 116
free-range, 39

French fries, 111
Frivolité de Saumon Fumée au Poireau
  et Fromage de Chèvre, 17
fruits
  Apples with Cinnamon Calvados
    Cream, 14
  Balsamic Rhubarb Compote, 67
  Bar-b-qued Pineapple, 7
  Blueberry Sauce, 88–89
  Caramelized Peaches and
    Raspberry Sorbet, Chocolate and
    Roasted Walnut Tart with, 100
  Peaches with Brandy, 146
  Pears Poached in Strawberry Wine
    with Orange Vinaigrette, Baby
    Spinach and Mushroom Salad
    with Gorgonzola Cheese and,
    84–85
  Pecan Pumpkin Torte, 125–126
  Roasted Apple Coulis,
    Cherrywood-Grilled Arctic Char
    with, 121
  Sour Apricot Juice, 99
  Strawberries in Red Wine with
    Fresh Cracked Pepper, 145
  Watermelon-Mango Salsa, Grilled
    Sea Bass with, 24
"fusion" cuisine, 30

garlic chili sauce, 35
Gatineau Hills (Quebec), 49
Gesti-Faune Inc., 18–19
ghee, 29
giblets, 42
Gnocchi alla Gorgonzola, 73
goat cheese, 52
goose. See poultry
gorgonzola, 73, 84
Graffiti, 12–14
La Grande Allee, 8
Gravy, 42
Gremolata, Lamb Shanks with Root
  Veggies, Mushrooms and, 53–54
Grilled Asparagus and Pork Salad, 4
Grilled Breast of Chicken Filled with
  Oka Cheese and Fresh Sage,
  96–97
Grilled Leg of Lamb, 3
Grilled Scallops with Sun-Dried
  Tomato Sauce, 58
Grilled Sea Bass with Watermelon-
  Mango Salsa, 24
Grilled Zucchini, Lemon, 6
grilling. See bar-b-ques

Hall, Nancie, 95
heli-hiking, 1–2
Herb Sauce, 91

herbs
  Chive Oil, Asparagus Soup with, 28
  Chive Oil, Chilled Smoked Salmon
    Soup with, 110–111
  Herb Sauce, 91
  Lemon Chive Oil, Roasted Lobster
    with, 81
  Rosemary-Parmesan Mashed
    Potatoes, 69
  Tarragon White Wine Sauce, 120
Homemade Ravioli Stuffed with
  Roasted Squash and Goat Cheese
  in Frangelico Butter Sauce,
  74–75

iceberg lettuce, 27

Juice, Sour Apricot, 99

Kamsack (Saskatchewan), 43–44
Key Lime Cheesecake Boisvert,
  124–125
Kindiak, Mary, 47
"Kitchen Jim," 139

Lac Portage, 18
Lac Portage Corporate Retreat,
  18–24
Lacroix, Jean-François, 19
lamb. See meats
Lamb Shanks with Root Veggies,
  Mushrooms, and Gremolata,
  53–54
Larousse Gastronomique, 92
Le St. Amour, 15–17
Leek and Mussel Soup, 117–118
legumes
  Cabbage Bean Soup, 46–47
  Lima Bean Salad, 13–14
  Three Bean Salad with Veggies, 138
Lemon Grilled Zucchini, 6
Lemon Vinaigrette, Chicken and
  Veggie Salad with, 134
Les Chefs des Chefs, 90
Lima Bean Salad, 13–14
Linguine with Clams, Tomatoes, and
  Arugula, 78
Longmire, Brian, 56

Malpeque Bay, 25
Manoir Brulé, 18
Marinated Asian Flank Steak, 36–37
Maritime Oyster Chowder with
  Telderberry Apple Wine and Sweet
  Curried Whipped Cream, 85–86

The Martooni Salad, 145
Matzala, Stella, 43
McNeil, George, 96
meats
    see also sweetbreads
    Beef and Pork Stew, 114–115
    The Best Ever Meat Loaf, 46
    Braised Short Ribs with Roasted
        Red Pepper and Red Wine Sauce,
        102–103
    Buffalo Eggplant Stew, 65
    Cipaille, 136
    Curried Lamb and Sweet Potato
        Stew, 135
    Grilled Asparagus and Pork Salad, 4
    Grilled Leg of Lamb, 3
    Lamb Shanks with Root Veggies,
        Mushrooms, and Gremolata,
        53–54
    Marinated Asian Flank Steak,
        36–37
    Pan-Fried Medallions of Veal
        Striploin with Telderberry
        Blueberry Wine Reduction and
        Sage Oil, 88–89
    patting dry, 105
    Penne with Sausages and Sun-
        Dried Tomatoes, 77
    Pork and Asparagus-Stuffed
        Parmesan Baskets, 109
    Pork Tenderloin in a Cassis
        Sauce, 113
    Roast Loin of Caribou Lac St. Jean
        with Smoked Corn and
        Buckwheat Croquette and Berry
        Chutney in Blueberry Poivrade,
        92–94
    Sassie de Caribou aux Petits Fruits
        des Marais, 15–16
    Steak and Frites with Honey-
        Buttered Carrots, 111
    Stuffed Veal Shoulder Roast in
        White Wine Reduction, 106–107
    Venison Shoulder Roast with
        Cranberry Cream Sauce, 62
    Vietnamese Beef and Shrimp
        Noodle Soup, 33
Moose, Bar-b-qued, 61
Most Excellent Fish Soup, 12–13
mushrooms
    Baby Spinach and Mushroom Salad
        with Gorgonzola Cheese and
        Pears Poached in Strawberry
        Wine with Orange Vinaigrette,
        84–85
    Bulgur Wheat and Wild Rice
        Risotto with Woodland
        Mushrooms, 97–98

Chicken Breasts Stuffed with Wild
    Mushrooms and Porcini Butter,
    50–51
cleaning, 51
dried, 50
Lamb Shanks with Root Veggies,
    Mushrooms, and Gremolata,
    53–54
mushroom filling, for perogies, 44
Mushroom Flan, Stefan's, 29
Penne with Mushrooms and
    Proscuitto, 79
Wild Mushroom and Goat Cheese
    Omelette, 52–53
wild porcini, 49–50
Mussel Soup, Leek and, 117–118
Mussels in Coconut and Lime
    Nectar, 123
Mussels with Cherry Tomatoes,
    Herbs and Cream, P.E.I., 118
Mussels with Garlic and Herbs,
    Super-Fast, 122

New Potato, Goat Cheese, and Green
    Bean Salad with Sweet Balsamic
    Vinaigrette, 68
Nichols, Dale, 83, 87
noodles. See pasta and noodles
The Nutty Trout, 22–23

Offer, Paul, 25
Ottawa Citizen, 140
Oyster Boy, 127–128
oyster po-boy, 130–131
oyster shucking, 127–128
oysters, 25–26, 85

Pan-Fried Medallions of Veal
    Striploin with Telderberry
    Blueberry Wine Reduction and
    Sage Oil, 88–89
Pan-Fried Oysters with Spicy Salsa,
    129
Pan-Roasted Potatoes, 104
Pan-Seared Breast of Duck in
    Soy-Honey Sauce, 142
Pan-Wilted Garlic Spinach, 104
pasta and noodles, 72–73
    Bugaboo Couscous, 6
    Bulgur Wheat and Wild Rice
        Risotto with Woodland
        Mushrooms, 97–98
    Cold Shrimp and Noodle Salad, 37
    Dim Sum Shrimp Dumplings with
        Three Dipping Sauces, 34–35
    Gnocchi alla Gorgonzola, 73

Homemade Ravioli Stuffed with
    Roasted Squash and Goat Cheese
    in Frangelico Butter Sauce,
    74–75
Linguine with Clams, Tomatoes,
    and Arugula, 78
Penne with Mushrooms and
    Proscuitto, 79
Penne with Sausages and Sun-
    Dried Tomatoes, 77
Tagliatelle al Pollo, 76
Vietnamese Beef and Shrimp
    Noodle Soup, 33
patting dry, 105
Peaches with Brandy, 146
Peanut Dipping Sauce, 35
pear, Anjou, 84
pear wine, 87
Pear Wine Butter Sauce, 87–88
Pecan Pumpkin Torte, 125–126
P.E.I. Mussels with Cherry
    Tomatoes, Herbs and Cream, 118
Pelican Fuillette with Tarragon
    White Wine Sauce, 119–120
The Pelican Grill, 116
Penne with Mushrooms and
    Proscuitto, 79
Penne with Sausages and Sun-Dried
    Tomatoes, 77
perogie fillings, 44–45
perogies, 43–46
Pineapple, Bar-b-qued, 7
The Pines, 56–57
piri piri sauce, 40
poaching, 83
Poppy Seed Cake, 48
pork. See meats
Pork and Asparagus-Stuffed
    Parmesan Baskets, 109
Pork Salad, Grilled Asparagus
    and, 4
Pork Tenderloin in a Cassis Sauce, 113
Potatoes, Pan-Roasted, 104
poultry, 38–39, 76
    The Basic Bird, 39–40
    Chicken and Veggie Salad with
        Lemon Vinaigrette, 134
    Chicken Ballentine with Carrot
        Butter and Beet Emulsions,
        26–27
    Chicken Breasts in Riesling
        Sauce, 105
    Chicken Breasts Stuffed with Wild
        Mushrooms and Porcini Butter,
        50–51
    Chicken in Whisky Peanut Sauce,
        144

Cinnamon Crust Breast of Turkey
    with Sweet and Spicy Thai Cream
    Sauce, 60–61
Cipaille, 136
Confit de Canard, Pommes à l'Ail, 11
giblets, 42
Gravy, 42
Grilled Breast of Chicken Filled
    with Oka Cheese and Fresh Sage,
    96–97
Pan-Seared Breast of Duck in
    Soy-Honey Sauce, 142
patting dry, 105
Pelican Fuillette with Tarragon
    White Wine Sauce, 119–120
Roast Goose with Two Stuffings,
    63–65
The Spicy Bird, 40–41
stuffing, 39
The Ultimate Bird, 41–42
Prairies, 73
presentation, 61
Prince Edward Island, 25–26
proscuitto
    Penne with Mushrooms and
        Proscuitto, 79
    Shrimp Flambé with Proscuitto, 140
Pumpkin Soup, 19–20
Pumpkin Torte, Pecan, 125–126

Quebec City, bistros, 8–9

Raspberry Sorbet, 100
Ratushny, Marg, 44
rice wine, 34
Riesling Sauce, Chicken Breasts
    in, 105
Roast Goose with Two Stuffings,
    63–65
Roast Loin of Caribou Lac St. Jean
    with Smoked Corn and
    Buckwheat Croquette and Berry
    Chutney in Blueberry Poivrade,
    92–94
Roasted Apple Coulis, Cherrywood-
    Grilled Arctic Char with, 121
Roasted Lobster with Lemon Chive
    Oil, 81
Roasted Red Pepper and Red Wine
    Sauce, Braised Short Ribs with,
    102–103
Rodney's Oyster Bar, 127–128
Rosemary-Parmesan Mashed
    Potatoes, 69
Rosowsky, Anna, 43, 44
roux, 42
Royal York, 95–96

Sage and Onion Stuffing, 64
sake, 34
salad
    Baby Spinach and Mushroom Salad
        with Gorgonzola Cheese and
        Pears Poached in Strawberry
        Wine with Orange Vinaigrette,
        84–85
    Buttermilk Slaw, 137
    Chicken and Veggie Salad with
        Lemon Vinaigrette, 134
    Lima Bean Salad, 13–14
    The Martooni Salad, 145
    New Potato, Goat Cheese, and
        Green Bean Salad with Sweet
        Balsamic Vinaigrette, 68
    Three Bean Salad with Veggies, 138
salsa
    Spicy Salsa, Pan-Fried Oysters
        with, 129
    Watermelon-Mango Salsa, Grilled
        Sea Bass with, 24
Sassie de Caribou aux Petits Fruits des
    Marais, 15–16
Sauce Beurre Blanc, Truite en Colère
    avec, 20–22
sauces
    Blueberry Sauce, 88–89
    Cassis Sauce, Pork Tenderloin in a,
        113
    Cinnamon Calvados Cream,
        Apples with, 14
    Cranberry Cream Sauce, Venison
        Shoulder Roast with, 62
    fish sauce, 33, 37
    Gravy, 42
    Herb Sauce, 91
    Peanut Dipping Sauce, 35
    Pear Wine Butter Sauce, 87–88
    piri piri sauce, 40
    Riesling Sauce, Chicken Breasts
        in, 105
    Roasted Red Pepper and Red Wine
        Sauce, Braised Short Ribs with,
        102–103
    Sauce Beurre Blanc, Truite en Colère
        avec, 20–22
    Sesame Ginger Dipping Sauce, 35
    Soy-Honey Sauce, Pan-Seared
        Breast of Duck in, 142
    Sun-Dried Tomato Sauce, Grilled
        Scallops with, 58
    Sweet and Sour Sauce, 35–36
    Sweet and Spicy Thai Cream Sauce,
        Cinnamon Crust Breast of
        Turkey with, 60–61
    Tarragon White Wine Sauce, 120
    Whisky Peanut Sauce, Chicken in,
        144

sauerkraut filling, for perogies, 45
Sausage Meat Stuffing, 64
Sausages and Sun-Dried Tomatoes,
    Penne with, 77
Schebywolok, Jennie, 46
Schulze, Marilyn, 66
Seasons in Thyme, 25–26
Sesame Ginger Dipping Sauce, 35
shellfish. See fish and shellfish
Shrimp and Noodle Salad, Cold, 37
Shrimp Flambé with Proscuitto, 140
Simpson, Judd, 143
Sisteron (France), 142
Skinny Oyster Po-Boy with Aioli and
    Chives, 130–131
Slaw, Buttermilk, 137
Smoked Salmon and Arctic Char
    Tartare with Herb Sauce, 91
Smoked Salmon Soup with Chive Oil,
    Chilled, 110–111
soups
    Asparagus Soup with Chive Oil, 28
    Cabbage Bean Soup, 46–47
    Chilled Smoked Salmon Soup with
        Chive Oil, 110–111
    Creamy Cold Cucumber and Bell
        Pepper Soup, 133
    Curried Squash Soup, 141
    Leek and Mussel Soup, 117–118
    Maritime Oyster Chowder with
        Telderberry Apple Wine and
        Sweet Curried Whipped Cream,
        85–86
    Most Excellent Fish Soup, 12–13
    Pumpkin Soup, 19–20
    Thai Spicy Coconut Soup (Tom Kha
        Gai), 32
    Vietnamese Beef and Shrimp
        Noodle Soup, 33
Sour Apricot Juice, 99
Soy-Honey Sauce, Pan-Seared
    Breast of Duck in, 142
The Spicy Bird, 40–41
Spinach, Pan-Wilted Garlic, 104
Squash Soup, Curried, 141
star anise, 33
Steak and Frites with Honey-
    Buttered Carrots, 111
Stefan's Mushroom Flan, 29
Strawberries in Red Wine with Fresh
    Cracked Pepper, 145
strawberry wine, 84
Stuffed Veal Shoulder Roast in White
    Wine Reduction, 106–107
stuffing, 39, 64–65
    Roast Goose, 63–65
    Sage and Onion Stuffing, 64
    Sausage Meat Stuffing, 64

Sun-Dried Tomato Sauce, Grilled
    Scallops with, 58
Sun-Dried Tomatoes, Penne with
    Sausages and, 77
Super-Fast Mussels with Garlic and
    Herbs, 122
Sweet and Sour Sauce, 35–36
Sweet and Spicy Thai Cream Sauce,
    Cinnamon Crust Breast of
    Turkey with, 60–61
Sweet Curried Whipped Cream, 86
Sweet Potato Stew, Curried Lamb
    and, 135
sweetbreads
    Calf's Liver with Bacon, Herbs,
        and Balsamic Vinegar, 70–71
    Foie Gras à l'Armagnac, 16

Tagliatelle al Pollo, 76
Tarragon White Wine Sauce, 120
Tartare aux Deux Saumons, 10
Tataryn, Arlene. See dessert
Telder, Bob, 83
Tequila Lime Butter, Bar-b-qued
    Oysters with, 131
Thai chili paste, 60
Thai ingredients, 32
Thai Spicy Coconut Soup (Tom Kha
    Gai), 32
Three Bean Salad with Veggies, 138
Thyne Valley, 25
Tom Kha Gai (Thai Spicy Coconut
    Soup), 32
Tomatoes in Basil Balsamic Butter,
    Corn and, 71
trouting, 18–19
truffles, 41
Truite en Colère avec Sauce Beurre
    Blanc, 20–22
turkey. See poultry
turmeric, 123

The Ultimate Bird, 41–42

Vancouver Island (B.C.), 66–67
veal. See meats
vegetables
    Baby Spinach and Mushroom Salad
        with Gorgonzola Cheese and
        Pears Poached in Strawberry
        Wine with Orange Vinaigrette,
        84–85
    Buttermilk Slaw, 137
    Corn and Tomatoes in Basil
        Balsamic Butter, 71
    Creamy Cold Cucumber and Bell
        Pepper Soup, 133

Curried Squash Soup, 141
Grilled Asparagus and Pork Salad,
    4
Homemade Ravioli Stuffed with
    Roasted Squash and Goat Cheese
    in Frangelico Butter Sauce,
    74–75
Honey-Buttered Carrots, Steak
    and Frites with, 111
Leek and Mussel Soup, 117–118
Lemon Grilled Zucchini, 6
New Potato, Goat Cheese, and
    Green Bean Salad with Sweet
    Balsamic Vinaigrette, 68
Pan-Roasted Potatoes, 104
Pan-Wilted Garlic Spinach, 104
Pumpkin Soup, 19–20
Rosemary-Parmesan Mashed
    Potatoes, 69
Three Bean Salad with Veggies, 138
Venison Shoulder Roast with
    Cranberry Cream Sauce, 62
Venturi, Giordano, 66
Venturi-Schulze winery, 66
Vietnamese Beef and Shrimp Noodle
    Soup, 33
vinegar, Aceto Balsamico, 66–67
Vintner's Quality Assurance,
    101–102
VQA, 101–102

Watermelon-Mango Salsa, Grilled
    Sea Bass with, 24
wheat, 72–73
Whisky Peanut Sauce, Chicken in,
    144
Wild Mushroom and Goat Cheese
    Omelette, 52–53
Wild Rice Risotto with Woodland
    Mushrooms, Bulgur Wheat and,
    97–98

Zucchini, Lemon Grilled, 6
zuppa di pesce. See Most Excellent
    Fish Soup